Striving *for* Significance

Life lessons learned while fishing

Other books by **Dave Romeo**

Stumbling Onto Success!
Turning Mistakes into Masterpieces
(Executive Books, 2006)

Designing Your Destiny
22 Steps to a Compelling Future
(iUniverse Publishing, 2003)

Nice Guys Finish <u>First</u>!
How to be a Winner <u>Without</u> Losing Your Integrity
(Primary Publishing, 2000)

Dave Romeo's Long Island Freshwater Fishing Guide
(Dave Romeo Publishing, 1990)

Better Bass Fishing - The Dave Romeo Way
(Sterling Publishing Co., Inc., 1988)

These books may be purchased by calling (717) 361-2418.

Striving *for* Significance

Life lessons learned while fishing

DAVE ROMEO

iUniverse, Inc.
New York   Bloomington

Striving for Significance
Life lessons learned while fishing

iUniverse books may be ordered through booksellers or by contacting:

iUniverse
1663 Liberty Drive
Bloomington, IN 47403
www.iuniverse.com
1-800-Authors (1-800-288-4677)

Because of the dynamic nature of the Internet, any Web
addresses or links contained in this book may have changed
since publication and may no longer be valid.

ISBN: 978-1-4401-2212-5 (pbk)
ISBN: 978-1-4401-2213-2 (ebk)

Printed in the United States of America

iUniverse rev. date: 2/19/2009

Lovingly Edited by Barb Kovalsky
Extraordinary Cover Design by Erin McRedmond
Priceless Cover Photo by Phil Garber
Final Manuscript Painstakingly Reviewed by Jody Osborne
Cherish Denton – Publishing Service Associate, iUniverse

Contents

About the Author

Dave Romeo was born in Brooklyn, New York and grew up in the little town of East Meadow on Long Island. In 1984, he established a Guinness World Record for the most fish caught in a season by catching 3,001 largemouth bass in 77 days of fishing. This achievement became a pivotal point in his life as it opened up a floodgate of opportunities.

Among these opportunities were Dave's first two books entitled: ***Better Bass Fishing - The Dave Romeo Way*** (Sterling Publishing Co., Inc., 1988) and ***Dave Romeo's Long Island Freshwater Fishing Guide*** (Dave Romeo Publishing, 1990).

Dave designed a series of bass fishing lures for Panther Martin Lures and starred in a full-length instructional bass fishing video entitled, ***Fish with the World's Greatest Bass Fisherman*** (Atlas Telecommunications, 1990). For ten years, he ran Dave Romeo Bass Tournaments. Eventually he decided to use what he learned from fishing and from running his own business to aid other business people.

In 1990, Dave moved to Lancaster County, Pennsylvania where he married Kim Trout, a Lancaster County native. He fell in love with Kim and the Lancaster culture simultaneously. The couple now resides in Elizabethtown, Pennsylvania.

In 1992, Dave became a staffing recruiter for the printing industry. In 1998, he became an owner at Primary Staffing Services in Lancaster, Pennsylvania. He heads the Primary Seminars & Coaching by Dave Romeo division, serving as a personal and professional results coach and an international motivational speaker, primarily in the areas of sales, leadership, and personal growth. Dave was influenced most significantly by Ken Blanchard, Dale Carnegie, Don Hutson, Harvey Mackay, John Maxwell, Tom Peters, Anthony Robbins, Lance Secretan, and Brian Tracy. He has read virtually every book written by these authors. Their influence can be felt in this book.

In 2000, he published his landmark book, ***Nice Guys Finish First! - How to Be a Winner Without Losing Your Integrity*** (Primary Publishing, 2000), establishing him as a powerful storyteller with a gift for inspiring readers.

In 2003, Dave published ***Designing Your Destiny - 22 Steps to a Compelling Future*** (iUniverse Publishing, 2003), which has become a field-manual for people who wish to improve their lives. Now also published in Chinese, ***Designing Your Destiny*** is one of more than fifty electrifying seminars presented by Dave Romeo.

In 2006, Dave published ***Stumbling Onto Success - Turning Mistakes Into Masterpieces*** (Executive Books, 2006). The book maps out many of the strategies that have made his seminars such a phenomenal success. ***Stumbling Onto Success*** delves deeply into the practice of goal setting (an area the author has mastered), thus making this book a world-wide smash. If you wish to obtain a FREE electronic version of the goal list contained in this book, please email Dave Romeo at daveromeo@embarqmail.com

In 2007, Dave achieved another fishing milestone. He caught, recorded, and released more than 25,000 bass in twenty-five years. This remarkable story generated many revelations about how you can take an ordinary activity to discover so many valuable lessons and use them in all different areas of your life. Many of these lessons have formed the basis of this book.

Dedication

First, the biblical story of *The Good Shepherd* on which I strive to model my life.

Second, to Mike Fenech. While on earth, you always had my back. Now that you are in Heaven, thank you for bringing even bigger blessings into my life. Congratulations on your promotion.

Third, to my wife Kim. Any growth that I have experienced over the past twenty years has been as a direct result of your positive influence on my life. Never have I known a person who so truly is the living embodiment of unselfishness, thoughtfulness, and consideration as you. There will probably never be another human being who can appreciate just how thoroughly you have enriched my life, and yet, as unworthy as I am, you do it anyway. Your love for me is the definition of true significance.

Acknowledgements

First and foremost, I express my complete thanks and appreciation to God for allowing me to pluck away at the keyboard for this book.

To my great family, especially my incredible parents Rita and Salvatore Romeo, my wonderful brother Jack and the rest of the Romeo, Trout, Caldeira, and Iskric clans. I love you all. Thanks for putting up with me.

I extend my appreciation to all of the members of Saints Peter and Paul Roman Catholic Mission in York, PA and in particular the Barry, Fonticoba, Kearney, Mackan, Noel, Pitman, Schriver, and Vargas families who have become such an endless source of inspiration. I am humbled to be in your company and I strive to be in your class.

Deepest thanks to the numerous *'knowledge sponges'* who attend my seminars with insatiable enthusiasm including: Carol Ann Agnew, John Anthony, Stephanie Aponte (*my customer service super hero*), Sheri Baer, Mary Balciar, Matthew Best, Elaine Bledsoe, Jackie Boyer, Kim Brenner-Zirkle, Hadley Brown, Roger Brubaker, Scott Brubaker, Nate Bunty, Matthew Byerly, Rhonda Campbell, Mel Carlton, John Carrigan, Terry Carver (***The Maestro of the Kitchen***), Doug Chew, Mike Clossey, Mike Coulson, Eric Davenport, Bruce Davis, Art Dean, Don DeHart, Raylene DeSanto, Ed Dickel, Jeff Dombach, Mike Donnelly, Maureen Dressman, John Evans, Cheryl Feeser, Mike Ferro, Karen Fink, Judy Franklin, Kevin Fry, Jim Gante, John Gill, Carol Glass, Clay Golden, Rae Jean Gracey, Kelli Grim, Cory Grimm, Crystal Grove, Chris Gumbert, Rob Hager, Beth Haldeman, Melynda Hasselbach (***my twin!***), Joe Heidler, Eric Hess, Susan Holtzinger, Wendell Hoover, Jason Hubler, Dan Irvin, Cathy Johnson, Bob Kandratavich, Carole and Rob Kaufhold, Ken Keifer, Paul Kohler, Kirby and Rene Kopp, Shay Kreider, John Leader, David Leedom, Lou Leyes, Dan and Melissa Lineaweaver, Bonnie Locher, Felecia Lundgren, Glenda Machia, Selina Man, Charlie Mann, Ronnie McComsey, Jana McGuire, Sharon McHarg, Bob and Rose Ann McRedmond, Erin McRedmond, Leon Miller (***both of them***), Stephen Morris, James Murphy, Fred Myers, Art Noel, Judy Ochs, Jody Osborne, Lisa Overly, Jill Parsons, John Platts, Jennifer Powell, Heather Pryor, Nicole Ream, Jill Reed, Cathy Ritter, David Ritter, Lee Roe, Jon and Lori Ruffner, Joyce Ruffner, Michelle Salinas, Karen Saxe, Nancy Seibert, Jennifer Senft, Terry Senft, Rose Shaffer, Tom Shotzbarger, Lisa Shrauder, Heather Shue, Stephen Sikking, Morrell Sipe, Beth Smith, Dwight Smith, Dave Spangler (***the other one***), Dave Stakem, Ron Stare, Beth and Hank Stauffer, Beth and Clark Tomlinson, Jeff Umberger, Mindy Valan, Mike Vargo, Angie Wagner, Paul Walk, Anne West, Randy

Whitfield, Kimberley Woods, Marcy Workman, David Young, Leah Young, and Darlene Zerbe. You've allowed me the privilege of enjoying the greatest job in the world. What would I ever do without you? I love you all dearly from the bottom of my heart.

Thanks to my mentors, coaches and colleagues including: (the late, great) David Boehm, Bob Buerger, Laura Douglas, Myron Golden, Becky and Jim Hoffman, Don Hutson, (the late) Charlie 'Tremendous' Jones, Father Denis McMahon, Sharon Mitzell, Mary Scoles, Steve Spangenberg, Father Gabriel Tetherow, Brian Tracy, and Annabelle Woodard. You have guided me well in more ways than you will ever know.

My great friends and role models including: Barbara and Tim Anglim, Bruce Cooper, Mike Fenech (recently departed), Art Gardner, Jasmine Grimm, Bernadette Hill, Mary Hoffman, Karen Johnson, Mark Kanterman, Barb Kovalsky (my fantastic editor), John Lastra, David McLaughlin, Billy Morrison, Peter Nicholson, Mike and Patti Jo Peters, Ray Pinto (gone but not forgotten), Jennifer Umberhocker, and Barb and Carl Wilson. Thanks for choosing to share your lives with me.

And also to Rick and Brenda Conley, Amanda Dodson, and the whole gang at Primary Staffing Services who make me *appear* respectable through my association with them.

Finally, a special thank you to all the networkers like: Brian Allen, Duane Dagen, Rodney Garber, Gerry Giberson, Kae Groshong-Wagner, Lon Heiser, Randy Jackson, Brian Jacobeen, Marvin Johnson, Kim Lutz, Dave

Spangler (***the first one***), Pete Wehler, and Gary Zimmerman for introducing me to landowners like: Tom Baldridge, Henry Barley, Paul Breneman, Cliff Charles, Bill Clayton, Phil Garber, Dean Herr, Bill Hess, George Kain, Jacob King, Tom Knaub, Dennis Kowal, Chris Kuntz, Dennis Metzler, Claire Miller, Red Musser, Cale Rafferty, Mary Anne Reedy, Andy Stoltz, Jack Stoner, James Strickler, Dave Sweigert, Terry Switzer, Derek Tatman, Polly Tobias, Joan Weaber, Van Winkle, and Stan Wojtusik who generously gave me permission to fish on their properties. Without you this book would not exist. Because of you I feel like I have glimpsed Heaven.

Foreword

Sometimes, life can feel so painfully frustrating, especially when we lose sight of its true meaning. So I can't help but to thank God for Dave Romeo's insight when I had to tangle with that horrible feeling myself.

When I met Dave, there was something about him that rekindled my own burning desire to achieve my goals. That's because he taught me how to look past my accomplishments to understand their significance. More importantly, though, he taught me how to deal with the empty feeling that often accompanies unsatisfying achievements.

I'm talking about the let down you sometimes feel after you accomplish something you sought out to do and the thrill begins to wear off. It's the moment after you are awarded a blue ribbon, win a wrestling match or, in Dave's case, the moment after he caught the last of his 25,000 bass to achieve his goal. You may have experienced it when you've busted your tail to lose twenty-five pounds, but when you step on the scale, you don't feel like a different person just because the number is smaller. It feels like the moment after you get a big promotion so much faster than you anticipated, or the day after your wedding day when it's all just a memory. Or, more extravagantly still, how Neil Armstrong must have felt about a month after walking on the moon. How do you top that?

But regardless of the magnitude of the goal, the toughest part about that feeling is that it's not what you expected. In your head you had this whole idea all built up about how it would unfold. You thought it would be this grandiose bang inside your heart, but in reality, it sounds more like a whisper.

It's the *'That's it?'* feeling. I'm referring to the shattering of expectations when you finally achieve something you once thought was impossible. And you say to yourself, 'This is not how I expected to feel.' Then, after staggering around emotionally for a few seconds, you ask yourself, 'What's next?'

When you, dear reader, are wrestling with this feeling, I would like to pass on a lesson Dave taught me. He told me to remind myself, '***What* I did** should be less important to me than **the fact that it *could* be done**.'

Dave taught me that even though it's the crummiest feeling in the world for an accomplishment to feel meaningless, whatever the goal may be, it was not won without great personal sacrifice, dedication, and harsh criticism. He taught me that the goal was significant because when I attempted my dreams, I did so despite the fact that they would be fraught with adversity, challenges, and setbacks.

He taught me what is significant is not that I achieved a goal, but rather, that I dared to try. He reminded me that the quest is what is truly meaningful. Once I learned and truly internalized the significance of this, Dave rekindled my drive to go after my goals.

Dave has that effect on people. He's the kind of person who walks into a room and you know somewhere within the pit of your stomach that your life is going to change because you met him.

He's someone who gives you this intrinsic feeling that you can go after your dreams. He's like the grown up version of that teacher you had as a little kid who told you that you could be anything you wanted. Dave holds you accountable to write down your goals and to go after them.

So what else can he teach you? Make it your goal to turn the page and find out.

- Jasmine Grimm

Prologue

'You are the sum of your decisions.'
- Anonymous

This is not a book about bass fishing, despite the cover photo. It is a book written by a bass fisherman and chronicles the lessons gained while fishing in solitude, being one with nature and alone with one's thoughts. What does one do out there, driving, walking, wading, and fishing for all those years? What significance could possibly be gained by such a venture? And, more importantly to you, my reader and my companion for the next 150 pages, what benefit could this book afford you in exchange for your intrepid time commitment? It is merely the knowledge and better understanding of yourself and the meaning of your existence.

It is in those quietest of moments when we are not plastered in front of a television screen or plopped down behind a desk that we discover life's most meaningful messages. This book was written to capture those precious lessons gleaned during the quiet stretches of undisturbed thought that have made up the past twenty-seven years of my life.

Do you ever spend any time alone-by yourself-on purpose? I believe some people are afraid to be by themselves for any considerable period of time. Yet, I spent a great part of the last quarter of a century standing in water, studying my surroundings, and negotiating with bass. What I sought while I pursued my angling passion was to understand the answers to life and to better understand the person I have become so far. It was a time of great introspection, fueled by a burning desire to become better at the things that matter: a better husband, a better Catholic, a better presenter, a better coach, a better role model, and, hopefully for your sake, a better author.

I don't believe we have the right to enjoy the precious God-given gift of life without making the most of this experience. I challenge you to make the most of this one-time opportunity and create an unforgettable ride that will provide fulfillment for you and those whose lives you touch.

This book is about you. It is about you discovering the important messages of life and creating an abundant existence for you and for others. It is about consciously making positive decisions that improve your life, learning from your mistakes, and embracing your faith.

> **'This book is about painting a masterpiece with your life.'**
> **- Dave Romeo**

Introduction: Got Purpose?

> *'Most people die when they're twenty-five
> and wait until they're seventy to be buried.'*
> *- Dave Ober*

It happened almost on cue. On August 11, 2005, I was driving down the road from my office to my home. It must have been close to six o'clock. I was thinking to myself about how pleased I was at having just put the finishing touches on my latest book (at the time), **Stumbling Onto Success!** There is a great sense of satisfaction that comes from publishing a new book. I imagine it is close to the experience of becoming a father, though I have no actual frame of reference on the latter. So, at the risk of me alienating any new fathers who might have picked up this book to give it a once-over, I still feel that the culmination of a three-year project, such as publishing a new book, is thrilling enough in its own right.

In any case, as I was casually driving down that particularly familiar stretch of Route 283 West in Lancaster County, Pennsylvania, my eye caught sight of an intriguing bumper sticker on the rear of a passing vehicle. It was just there for a brief instant, but it was long enough to accomplish its mission. As the purple Kia automobile whizzed by me on the right, I glanced over and read its two-word question. The bumper sticker simply read, *'Got Purpose?'*

In an instant, that small foreign car was gone, but that question has remained with me ever since that day. It's been years since I read that bumper sticker, and yet the message is as relevant today as it was when I first read it. I have not seen or heard of another bumper sticker with the same message, although certainly hundreds, or perhaps even thousands, of them must exist somewhere. Yet, the uniqueness of that challenging question at the exact same time I was contemplating the topic for this, my next book, has not been lost on me. In fact, it was the exact message I had planned to explore. After all, **success is all well and good, but what is success when compared to significance?**

There is a strange feeling that comes over an author (well, this author anyway) as soon as one completes a book. It is as if you stop to say, 'Now what? Is this all there is? Will what you just wrote change the world? Is it not the same world that existed before you wrote this book? *What is the purpose?'*

So you see, there it is. **That same message that sped by me in August of 2005 is the same question I ask of you now.** *What is the purpose of your life?* **What will you make of it and how will you achieve significance in the one brief lifespan with which you have been gifted?** Let us go now in search of it together.

Chapter 1: That Confounded License Plate

'We make the journey, but
God makes the path.'
- Dave Romeo

People often ask me why I decided to pursue being the first person to ever catch, record, and release 25,000 bass in a lifetime. Granted, it was an unusual pursuit. I'm sure I would ask the very same question if I heard of someone else going after such an outrageous milestone. To dedicate more than half of your life (twenty-seven years to be precise) to a passion (not a profession or, necessarily, a money-making exploit) should naturally spark some curiosity. I wish I could tell you that it all began with some grand master plan, but to borrow a line from my last book, it all began by way of stumbling onto success…and one very annoying license plate.

Around 1994, my wife decided to get a special license plate for her Saturn automobile because some of the money went to support Pennsylvania's wildlife. Since both Kim and I love animals, it seemed like a worthwhile contribution. She asked me if I wanted to get a special plate or vanity plate too since she was placing her order. I thought about it and, since it was for a good cause, I agreed, but I didn't know what to put on my plate. Originally I thought maybe '3001 BASS' in reference to my Guinness World Record. (In 1984, I caught 3,001 largemouth bass in 77 days of fishing which, to this day, is still the current record for the most fish caught in a season.) But by 1994, I had just caught my 10,000th bass, so I decided to go with '10K BASS.'

Unfortunately, when I got my new vanity plate in the mail, it was apparent that something had gotten lost in the translation. My plate read '1 OK BASS.' I put it on my car and from then on I was constantly answering the same annoying question: 'What does **one OKAY bass** mean?' Well, of course it didn't mean anything. It was a mistake, but I still had to go through the same frustrating explanation.

I attempted to get the error corrected, but as you might expect, it took quite a long time to clearly communicate my intended message to the Department of Motor Vehicles. I finally got the matter resolved and received a corrected license plate. Ironically, not long after I put on my new license plate, my car was hit from behind on an icy highway and both the car and the license plate were totaled. I needed to get yet another license plate to replace my now crumpled one.

For some strange and timely reason, the DMV sent me a letter saying that they wanted to make sure that my license plate message was correct and that if it was not, I could change it at no charge. By the time I finally got the matter resolved and received my accurate license plate,

I had caught over 13,000 bass. Well, I wasn't about to put '13K BASS' on my plate, so I decided I would give myself a little cushion. I figured if I picked a number so **outrageously** high, I wouldn't have to worry about actually hitting it or changing my license plate again. I requested that the license plate read '25K BASS.' There. Now that's settled. I never dreamed of ever reaching that number. But something happens in your subconscious when you are continually looking at the same message over and over again. At some point, it just became sort of a self-fulfilling prophesy—a pursuit that would take over a quarter of a century to complete.

Lesson: **There are sign posts that will guide us on our path towards significance, if we would just learn to recognize them.** I'm sure the events in my life unfolded exactly as they were supposed to. It just took me a little while to realize it. The same is true in *your* life. **You may not yet realize that the crosses you sometimes bear are not punishments but a means for you to achieve an outcome greater than your wildest dreams.** Instead of resisting them, recognize the challenges and growth opportunities they will provide you.

But I'm getting ahead of myself. Let me bring you back to the beginning of my bass fishing fascination—a brief conversation in the most unlikely of settings which would ignite a passion I didn't even know I had.

> *'Sometimes real life is just too small.*
> *You have to learn how to make it bigger.'*
> *- Dave Romeo*

Chapter 2: The Point of No Return

*'What mighty contests rise
from trivial things.'
- Alexander Pope*

Have you ever noticed how many seemingly insignificant and unpleasant incidences wind up becoming the basis for profound turning points in your life? I believe it is by design. You ask for a blessing and receive a problem. However, as you begin to dig in and solve that problem, you discover that inside it is the blessing you asked for in the first place. It may not look the way you expected it to look, but there it is.

It has been this way all of my life. I've gotten to the point where I don't even flinch when something negative occurs because, no matter what it brings, I end up learning from the challenge and becoming a better person from having tackled it.

The advantage of receiving your blessings disguised as problems is that you are forced to grow in the process. Hence, many times the knowledge gained in solving a problem you might not otherwise have faced becomes a gift.

In 1980, my grandfather August Romeo died. The significance of his funeral was that it reconnected me with several members of my family whom I hadn't seen in many years. One of them was my Uncle Eddie. Edward, my father's younger brother, moved away from New York in 1965. I hadn't seen him in fifteen years. He now lived in Ocala, Florida.

The night before he returned back home, Uncle Eddie regaled me with some incredible stories about bass fishing. I can still see him sitting on the bottom step of our home going on and on with exciting stories, one more incredible than the other, for my entertainment. I was captivated and hung onto his every word as he described vivid encounters with largemouth bass. That was my turning point. I was hooked before I ever caught a single bass, and there was no going back.

Since I lived in a landlocked county, almost all of my fishing experiences, up until that point, were limited to places I could only reach by bike. That meant, despite living on an island, I was fishing for freshwater species; and East Meadow, New York was never known as a hot spot for bass fishing. So, while I attended college I took a job working as a part-time driver for a flower shop.

The best thing about the job was that I drove all over Long Island and learned how to use a map. As I drove I noticed many intriguing bodies of water. After making my deliveries, I would drive past these bodies of water to see if there were any public access sites and then come back on my days off and fish them.

From that point on my life would be connected with bass fishing. So be it. Yet it was only the beginning of what became a twenty-seven-year pursuit that would transform me from a novice freshwater angler to a Guinness World Record Holder for bass fishing and a goal-driven individual.

Lesson: **No matter what you're doing, pay attention to what is going on around you.** That part-time job turned out to be one of the most significant I have ever held. Although I originally took the job to pick up some extra money while I was going to school, the long-lasting value was not the meager salary, but the discovery and awareness of the more than five-hundred freshwater bodies on Long Island. If you ask most people about fishing on Long Island, they will almost assuredly tell you about the excellent striped bass, bluefish, and fluke fishing available in the surrounding saltwater outskirts. Yet, many of these same aficionados don't have a clue about the spectacular freshwater bass fishing on Long Island. In addition, this opportunity added to my knowledge and allowed me to publish my second and, to date, still my best-selling book entitled *'Dave Romeo's Long Island Freshwater Fishing Guide.'*

Lesson: **Do the opposite. Sometimes, you need to ignore where everybody else is going and find your own path.** At the time, the population of Long Island was roughly equal to that of the entire state of Massachusetts. In addition, about one out of every three people on Long Island owned a boat. While almost everyone else did the same thing (saltwater fishing) I sought out an alternative passion where I practically had some of New York's best untapped bass fishing locations all to myself.

Lesson: **Sometimes the things you least want to do can benefit you in ways that you never imagined.** If it wasn't for my grandfather's funeral, I wouldn't have heard my uncle who ignited the spark of bass fishing in me, and the course of my life from that point on would have been altered dramatically.

> *'I fell in love with fishin' hook, line,*
> *and sinker...it was love at first bite.'*
> *– Anonymous*

Chapter 3: '39

'Tell me who you hang around with
and I'll tell you who you are.'
- Burke Hedges
(and his mom)

When I first began bass fishing, I decided I would record my daily fishing productivity so I could gauge my
progress. At the end of that first season, I had caught 39
bass.

How embarrassing! Imagine fishing all summer long
and only catching 39 bass! That was certainly not a very
impressive start. I remember reading about how Doug
Hannon, **the Bass Professor,** had caught more than 500
bass-each over ten pounds! Obviously, I knew I had a lot
to learn about bass fishing.

One thing I did learn was to avoid fishing with toxic
people. One in particular was **Joe the Weatherman.**
This was my nickname for a man I ran into often when I
started fishing. For a while, we would go fishing together. Joe knew a great deal about bass fishing, especially
about proper fishing gear usage and lure techniques. He

also had his own boat, which I did not. He was a much more skilled angler and had been at it longer than me.

I called him *Joe the Weatherman* because he would spend most of our fishing time together looking up at the sky and trying to convince me that it would either rain that day or the next. Why was he so obsessed with the weather? I'm not sure, but what I was sure of was that Joe was one of the most negative people I had ever encountered. He also taught me that **negative people don't like other people to be positive.**

I fished with Joe because he enjoyed bass fishing as much as I did and I figured I could learn how to become a better angler. Instead, he would unleash an endless stream of negativity to the point where my other friends did not want to fish with me if Joe was part of the group. My fishing productivity actually *worsened* when I was around Joe. Eventually, I had to cut the cord on that relationship. It was one of the few instances where I can remember doing that; but I've since learned that **if you only have one life to live, you are responsible for making the most of it. Don't waste a moment because you will never get it back.**

I'm guessing you and I were probably raised the same way. If you saw someone who was in need of help, you would naturally try to help the person. That core value makes it hard to leave someone, even if it is the right thing to do. In speaking with Dan Irvin yesterday, a protégé whom I've now known for over a decade, I mentioned '*The Ocean Liner Metaphor*' which I use to determine when enough is enough. It goes like this: if I'm out at sea on an ocean liner, and I see you in the water fighting for your life to stay afloat, I'll throw you a life preserver. If your response is to look at it and scoff, 'Oh, that's a white one. I wanted a blue one,' and you drown, I can live with myself.

This metaphor has come in very handy over the years because, when you are a coach, people come to you seeking help. Yet, not everyone who comes will do anything to improve his or her life. If you decide to **waste your time** helping people who do not want to improve their lives, you will be denying **the investment of your time** to others more serious about bettering themselves.

I also mentioned to Dan that when you encounter someone who is drowning in quicksand, one of two things is likely to happen. Either you'll pull him out or he's going to pull you in, so make sure that you are standing on solid footing. I've learned that sometimes, people are pretty comfortable treading quicksand because it adds legitimacy to and sympathy for their complaints. You'd better decide in advance which of you is more likely to outlast the other. The sooner you learn this reality, the less pain you will experience in your life and the further you will go.

I wasn't happy with my thirty-nine bass season, but there was nothing I could do about it. John Maxwell says, 'Everyone who ever got where they are started from where they were.' That's as true for me as it is for you. Besides, **you don't drown from falling in water; you drown from staying there.**

Lesson: I don't blame my embarrassing thirty-nine bass season on Joe. That was a result of my actions. I chose to allow Joe's negativity to affect me. Although I waited longer than I should have, eventually I recognized that he would not become more positive around me; however, I might become more negative around him. According to motivational speaker Ed Foreman, 'All the water in the world can't sink a ship unless it gets on the inside.' **Take care not to let the negativity around you get inside. Make good choices, especially when it comes to selecting your friends. It's better to have a couple of true blue friends you can depend on than 39 toxic ones who just want someone to be miserable with.**

Ironically, that number 39, which haunted me back in the early days of my bass fishing career, would later hold a much more positive significance. As we continue on this journey, you'll see what I mean.

> *'I hear and I forget. I see and I remember. I do and I understand.'*
> *- Chinese Proverb*

Chapter 4: Take the Long Way Home

'Success is to be measured not so much
by the position one has reached in
life as by the obstacles which one has
overcome while trying to succeed.'
– Booker T. Washington

A recent television advertising campaign by the office supply company Staples features an *'easy'* button where people just press it and instantly their problems are solved. They even sell *'easy'* buttons in their stores. If you hit the *'easy'* button, you'll hear a voice say, 'That was easy.' It sure would be nice to have a real *'easy'* button for those times when we're having a hard time coping with some of life's challenges.

Have you ever wondered why life can be so difficult sometimes? Little aggravations occasionally get the best of us. It's amazing how little it takes to distract us from what is truly important. Flat tires, lost car keys, and burnt toast seem like major catastrophes when they happen to us, especially when we're running late for something important. Yet, if we look closer, we will see that there are some very valuable lessons we can take from life's minor inconveniences. In fact, without them we might never develop our full potential.

As I have previously mentioned, in 1984, I established a Guinness World Record by catching 3,001 largemouth bass in 77 days of fishing. I learned a lot in a short period of time, but I still had more lot to learn. For example, the most bass I caught in one day was 99. I can still remember staying out there on that warm July night fishing until a quarter to ten, desperately trying to catch one more bass and achieve triple digits, but to no avail. I tried many times over the years without success to catch 100 or more bass in a single day. My fishing buddies would even take me out and try to help me hit this goal, but without success. Ironically, they would occasionally surpass the 100 bass in a one-day threshold while I fell short of the mark.

Some days, I would get a late start because I'd be stuck doing hours of much-dreaded yard work. Don't get me wrong. I love that my wife Kim and I own our own home, but the upkeep on our land is brutal, and I don't just mean the grass. We have these landscaped islands filled with all types of evergreen trees, holly bushes, and more kinds of greenery than I could name (*if I knew their names*, which I don't, and never cared to learn).

And then there's that dreaded hill at the end of our driveway. You see, when we first bought our property there was no house on it, so we did not know exactly what our home would look like until after it was built. Because our property sits on a ridge, the front yard is fifteen feet higher than the backyard, leaving a huge chunk of yard unmowable. This meant that we had to slope the ground between the driveway and the backyard to prevent a sheer drop-off, thus creating 'the hill.'

We tried covering the hill with Blue Rug Juniper bushes and all kinds of other shrubbery, but it was still a nightmare to maintain. It seemed to be a weed magnet. I can't calculate how much of my valuable fishing time I lost to weeding that huge sloping monstrosity. And the entire time I would be pulling and spraying weeds, I'd be thinking to myself about how many bass I could be catching if weren't stuck doing that never-ending yard work. (Just consider this a word to the wise or, more likely, to anyone who happens to marry someone with a green thumb. All I can say is *'it must be love.'*) Back at that time, my only appreciation for gardening came from taping two sets of foam kneeling cushions together and using them to prevent my car-top bass boat from scratching the roof of my automobile.

Ironically, even with the late starts, I'd still sometimes catch as many as 87 bass and think, 'If I come back here tomorrow, first thing in the morning, and fish straight through the day, surely I'll catch over 100 bass in one day.' Yet, without fail, something would change (weather conditions, location of floating vegetation, other anglers fishing there, or just less cooperative bass) and I would repeatedly fail to hit the century mark each time. What a cruel joke!

Falling short of my goal was most frustrating when I knew of places that would be red hot and I'd be prevented from fishing by the stipulations of the private property landowners. One owner only allowed me to fish his ponds on Saturdays, even though I usually fished on Sundays or Mondays. He would not budge. Another only let me fish his pond if I would stop after I caught five bass. That would take about ten minutes to accomplish. A new neighbor refused to return my calls when he bought a nearby property and pond which produced high numbers of bass all year long on a variety of lures even when they weren't biting anyplace else. It was a major strategic blow.

It was frustrating knowing I could accomplish my goal so much easier and faster if I only had their consent. All that time I kept thinking, 'I could be back with my wife, not missing another dinner together, not missing another opportunity to sit out together and watch the sunset from the comfort of our own deck.' It seemed so senseless. There were so many ways it could have been easier. Why did it have to be so hard? What was the point?

Another challenge I faced when I first got started was that despite catching large numbers of bass, I didn't catch many really large fish. A nineteen-inch bass, for example, weighs about four pounds. In the Long Island, New York area where I grew up, as in central Pennsylvania where I currently reside, that would be considered 'a lunker.' Yet when I began bass fishing, I only landed a handful of bass that size.

At the same time, I met a man who was about fifteen years older than me who was an incredible bass fisherman. He specialized in catching very big fish, regardless of the species. I saw evidence of his prowess firsthand, so I knew he was really talented. I only met him a couple of times, but I found him to be very unfriendly. What I remember most about him was his unwillingness to share his knowledge of how he caught those larger fish.

It was difficult for me to fathom why someone who was so gifted would hoard information about his experience. After all, he would still have all of his ability if he shared it with someone else, yet he was completely unwilling to part with any of his hard-earned knowledge. Life is loaded with enough struggles to go around. I thought to myself, 'Why must we deliberately make the path of our fellow men even more trying than necessary?'

I never did understand that angler's unwillingness to share his wisdom. Maybe he feared losing his superiority if someone else could duplicate his abilities. Perhaps it was jealousy. Whatever his reasons, they have remained a mystery to me to this day. Yet, what I do know is this: it's taken me nearly 25 years to equal his bass-fishing prowess. I can now catch bass of similar size with regularity. There were no shortcuts involved. Perhaps none ever existed. After all, who's to say that even if he had shared his secrets with me all those years ago that I would have been able to duplicate his results?

According to A.J. McClain, 'Learning to catch fish is not difficult, but becoming reasonably expert at it does require time and study.' My own results bore out that statement. I cannot tell you the exact day that I went from being an average angler to being an exceptional angler. It would be like asking Tiger Woods to tell you the precise day that he went from being an average golfer to being a world-class golfer. The answer lies in incremental steps, each so insignificant that we can hardly distinguish our individual improvements. Yet, if we string enough of them all together in a row for a long enough time, they can transform even our most mediocre attempts into significant accomplishments.

I use a similar example when a new coaching client is ready to hire me. It goes like this: 'I can give you a violin, but it won't make you a violinist. You will still need to practice long and hard with discipline, dedication, and follow-through in order to achieve the results you seek.' The same would be true for you, regardless of your choice of passion, task, or career.

Which of Thomas Edison's more than ten-thousand failed attempts to invent the electric light bulb was the most significant? And could he have discovered this breakthrough sooner if he had tried his final and successful attempt first? It seems unlikely that this would have happened because if the answer had been so obvious, someone else may have beaten him to that discovery.

Edison also, it seems, found no shortcuts. But then, look at all he gained by going the distance. For one, this man is now regarded as one of history's most prolific inventors with nearly fifteen-hundred patents to his credit. Certainly today he is considered one of the smartest men who ever lived. He improved the lives of countless millions of people across the globe through his discoveries which led to so many modern conveniences. I believe he understood that **the price of success is earned through our willingness to endure countless failures.** In addition, his legacy has become one of persistence for every other inventor, explorer, and scientist who have followed him. Consider, also, how his ideas will inspire new inventors to take the next logical steps in the development of break-through technology for future generations. **Improving the world for all who come after you—this is true significance.**

Lesson: There are no *'easy'* buttons, quick fixes, or shortcuts to achieving true significance because, as John Maxwell accurately reminds us, *'Success is not measured by what we get from it, but by what we become by it.'* **In other words, how will you be different or better as a result of attaining your accomplishments and, more importantly, by what you had to endure in order to achieve them? Therein lies your significance. It is not just the result of your outcome, but more so from your willingness to endure all of the disappointments, challenges, and failures that are inherent in achieving anything truly meaningful. It's a fact: we learn infinitely more from our setbacks than from our successes. We learn humility, patience, and persistence. And perhaps, most importantly, we discover just how truly committed we are to achieving our goals.**

I love this quote from Austrian chef and restaurateur, Wolfgang Puck, who said, *'I learned more from my one restaurant that didn't work than from all the ones that were successes.'* **There is your lesson. Don't fear**

making mistakes. Look forward to gaining experience and growing in knowledge. In fact, it was Zane Grey who said, *'I can learn from anyone, but I do not stop at that. I go on trying to learn from myself.'*

By the way, on May 28, 2006, I finally caught 116 bass in one day-- 22 years after getting into the Guinness Book of World Records. And it was ***worth*** the wait! Ironically, since that day I have been able to produce triple-digit daily bass scores four times in less than a month and eight times altogether. In fact, it took 22 years to go from catching 99 bass to catching 116 bass, but only nine days to go from catching 116 bass to 133 bass. The only difference was I now possessed the belief and the confidence that it could, indeed, be done.

I also landed 50 bass nineteen inches or longer in 2007, breaking my previous record high of 20 in 2004. Criswell Freeman claims that, *'The most important lure, remain the knowledge and ingenuity of the fisherman.'* I believe that statement transcends angling and applies to *all* life lessons.

Lesson: **It's amazing to learn what we are capable of once we have removed our own self-imposed limitations.**

> *'The man who keeps everything locked*
> *up in his heart will know far less than he*
> *who compares notes with his fellows.'*
> *- Theodore Gordon*

*You may have noticed by now that some of the chapter titles in this book are taken from song titles. I selected them for many different reasons, but primarily because they set the appropriate tone for their respective chapters. Also since, as you will see in subsequent chapters, music has played such an important part in my life, I thought this would be a nice tie-in. You will probably recognize some of the titles on your own; but if you would like a complete key to this book's chapter titles, I will make the answer key available to you.

To get a FREE electronic version of ***Striving for Significance: The Story Behind the Chapter Titles***, just e-mail me at: <u>daveromeo@embarqmail.com</u> and ask for 'SFS Chapter Titles.'

Chapter 5: No One to Run With

'For everything you have missed, you have gained something else and for everything you gain, you lose something else…to map out a course of action and follow it to an end requires courage.'
– Ralph Waldo Emerson

When I really started getting serious about bass fishing, one of the problems I encountered was finding places to fish that weren't over-crowded. While I was running fishing tournaments, it was easy to find people who wanted to go fishing with me. Even in Pennsylvania, almost all of my friends and in-laws fished. Many of them had their own boats. But as the years passed, one fact became very clear—I was the only one left from that group who was still bass fishing.

Fishing by myself didn't really bother me. Quite the contrary, the longer I did it, the better I became. It allowed me the opportunity to collect my thoughts, sharpen my focus, and pick up on many intricate details that would have escaped my notice had I been distracted by companions. Still, I couldn't help but wonder if perhaps

I might be the one who was missing out on something important.

Why was I the only one still at this? Had I missed the boat? Or was everyone else missing it because they could not go the distance? When I catch that final bass—number 25,000—will anyone else even know? And will it matter? I could not know the answer until I completed my quest. Only then would I be able to determine if my self-induced drive to fulfill that goal would be worth the price I would pay for all the sacrifices made by myself and everyone around me.

Lesson: Many of the greatest people in history spent at least a portion of their lives in solitude and loneliness. They suffered scorn and ridicule. People like Job, Noah, Moses, Abraham, Christopher Columbus, George Washington, Abraham Lincoln, Cole Porter, Helen Keller, Thomas Edison, and Alex Haley. Greatness is not without its price. And as Tony Robbins reminds us, *'There is no greatness without a passion to be great.'* **Just remember that even when you feel like an outcast and the most alone, God will be right by your side to see you through whatever must be endured. Use that peace to make the best possible decisions and do not worry if the world labels you a fool. Trust me—many of your labelers will most assuredly be fools themselves.**

Lesson: **At some point in your life, you will have to make some very hard choices and decisions.** You cannot have everything that you want. You will always have to trade off something for something else-whether it's time, money, companionship, integrity, position, or happiness. But **whatever you decide, hold on to your hope and confidence in God and believe that He will see you through to your destiny, no matter who else turns his or her back on you during your noble pursuits.**

'How vain it is to sit down to write
when you have not stood up to live.'
- Henry David Thoreau

Chapter 6: While You See a Chance

**'The brave may not live forever, but
the cautious do not live at all.'
- Philippe Renaldi
(from 'The Princess Diaries')**

One day, while I was feverishly racing from one fishing spot to another, I encountered a really difficult intersection where I needed to turn left. I had a stop sign and the cross traffic was very heavy. There were many cars behind me all coming off the same exit ramp of a major highway. You also couldn't easily see very far to the right, so I waited both patiently and anxiously to turn.

After a few minutes, the car behind me swerved to the left and then pulled up almost even with my driver's side window. I thought he wanted to get my attention, so I lowered my window. Instead he was just trying to make a left turn and was tired of waiting for me. He looked at me and just said, 'Sometimes you just have to take a chance.'

In the next moment, he was through the intersection and down the road to the left where I was planning to go. As I sat there, I realized that I was probably being overly cautious. I thought about what he said. How strange that a relationship, lasting for no more than a one-sentence monolog, could have such a significant meaning. I realized that he was right, and not just about making that left. In life we often have to be willing to take risks that don't come with guarantees. Sometimes we will succeed; other times we will fall short. But **it is in the willingness to take the risks that we truly discover what we are capable of achieving.**

I took away a lot from that brief interaction. I examined my life to see what kind of risks I was taking and reevaluated them. Some were reasonable, but others were far too cautious.

When I was in high school, my friends and I used to tease my best friend Art Gardner about his mother. Whenever he would tell his mother he was going somewhere, she would ask him, 'Is it safe?' The reason we found this so amusing is because Artie was the strongest kid in the entire school. He was also extremely resourceful and a bit of a daredevil. I remember him telling me years later, after he moved to Florida, that he was going to accompany a friend of his that night and catch alligators!

Artie had so many varied interests that were different than mine, and he never worried about what other people thought of him. As a result, he has since become incredibly knowledgeable concerning a great many subjects about which, to this day, I remain ignorant. He continues to amaze me with his ability to hold a conversation on so many different topics with anyone he meets.

Because his father died before we met in eighth grade, Artie had to be the surrogate dad to his two younger brothers. And while he didn't have a father around to hold his reckless side in check, he held himself in check and taught me a great deal. He became the first of my friends to get a job, a driver's license, a car, and to get married.

I'll admit that married life and raising children has mellowed Artie a bit, but what I admire most about him is his fearlessness and his willingness to learn about new things that I, most likely, would never have learned on my own. Artie has always been one of my role models, probably because, even though he is only nine months older than me, he taught me so much about life. It's amazing how someone who went to the same small private school with me for five years could have such an infinitely deeper knowledge of so many different areas of life than I did. This happened as a result of Artie not being afraid to try new things, a habit I still struggle to break.

As a result, I've adopted the three most valuable lessons I gleaned from Artie—taking personal responsibility, taking occasional risks, and being open to pursuing a wide variety of subjects such as: bass fishing, goal-setting, writing, painting, presenting seminars, coaching, personal relationships, weight loss, and financial planning. As I look back over my life, all of my associations with Artie have been for the better. Everyone should have a best friend like him.

Lesson: **It's time to examine your own life. Are you leading a life of quiet desperation? Have you taken some chances lately to broaden your horizons? While it's true that we need to strike a balance in all things, it is the passion we ignite that makes life less of an existence and more of an adventure.**

That motorist was right. **If you want to be successful, you cannot wait until everything falls into place. You will have to take chances to get what you want. The stronger your commitment to a cause, the more willing you are to take risks. In the moments of greatest adversity, it will be our willingness to take chances and see our outcomes through to completion that will determine how we look back over our lives.** Will it be with regret or with fulfillment? The choice is yours. Amen.

'Don't hide your light under
a bushel basket.'
- Origin Unknown

Chapter 7: One Day More

'Carpe Diem! Seize the day, put
no trust in the morrow!'
- Horace

One of my protégés, Erin McRedmond, suggested that I keep a fishing journal for my own benefit to record this amazing adventure. I said that I had been mentally doing it all along. In fact, the entire time I fished I did so imagining I was listening to sports commentators discussing every step along the way. It kept me on my toes and helped me maintain an extremely high level of intensity because I was continually striving to improve my performance. However, I thought you might like to see what it felt like as the twenty-seven-year journey neared its finale.

August 25, 2007. This is **the** day. Today, **I *will* catch and release bass number 25,000.** Only 26 bass remain. All things have come together in harmony to achieve the long-awaited final goal. I awoke on cue at 5:00 AM without an alarm clock. The car keys do not clang this morning because I remembered to pick them up in a clump so I would not wake my wife again. The cooler is packed to perfection: six slices of bread, five bottles of water, four bananas, four yogurts, four peaches, and four dry ice packs to endure the 90 degree temperature forecasted for today.

Knowledge is cumulative. Everything I have learned in the past twenty-seven years is being called upon to achieve the task at hand. The car is packed and waiting. Six fully-loaded rods and reels, oiled and respooled with new fishing line, are at the ready. Supplies of all lures (plastic worms and spinner baits mostly) have been restocked to make sure I won't run out of anything I'll need today.

All of today's primary and secondary fishing locations have been mapped out. Landowners' phone numbers are in place. The gas tank is full. All fishing gear has been cleaned and organized. All anticipated possibilities have been addressed and I am prepared to deal with all unforeseeable conditions as they arise including inclement weather, new 'no trespassing' signs, traffic jams, and vicious dogs.

There will be no faltering. I anticipate the unexpected so I will, therefore, be prepared to succeed despite any and all difficulties and challenges that might come my way. Nothing will stop me today but me. What am I doing here? It is time to go. It is time to meet my destiny! *Go!*

Lesson: **God gives you the tools, the opportunity, and the inspiration to accomplish what you will with your life. You are responsible for the execution required to deliver those results. Don't put it on anyone but yourself to succeed.**

*'Knowledge is not power. Knowledge
plus action, plus disciplined
follow-through is power.'
– Dave Romeo*

Chapter 8: If I Could Turn Back Time

'You can change your world if you want to.'
- 'Lucky' Horses - 1983

Do you believe that one can change the future by altering one's past? Most people would probably say 'no' and, until 2007, I would have most likely been among them. But I now had a good reason to ponder that question. It was an answer that I deeply wanted to learn.

They say that good things come in threes. In bass fishing, catching 3,001 bass in 77 days and getting into the Guinness Book of World Records was the first significant event in my life connected to bass fishing. I would not be the same person I am today had that incident never occurred. Incidentally, in order to catch 3,001 bass in 77 days, one must average 39 bass per day.

Now, I was approaching the second major bass fishing milestone: catching and releasing my 25,000th bass. It was a day I had looked forward to seeing for so long and it was now within my grasp, six years ahead of my initial projection.

Yet, even before the 25,000th bass was caught, there was one thought that kept running through my mind:

'25,000 bass in 27 years.' By the time I catch the 25,000[th] bass, I will have caught 7,550 bass in the previous four years. Had I only known that I could consistently catch over 1,100 bass a year (this happened seven out of the last eight years I fished), perhaps I could have caught **25,000 bass in 25 years.** It certainly had a better ring to it. But what could I do about it now? After all, what's done is done.

Now, more than ever, those measly 39 bass caught in 1981 were coming back to haunt me. And let's not forget about the paltry 147 bass in 1982. Had I not performed so poorly in those first two seasons, I could have surely caught 25,000 bass in 25 years. But wait! If I am now averaging over 65 bass per day, I could make up the combined 186 bass from those first two years in another three or four days. And, if I were to catch one more bass for every year I fished (27 bass), **I will have averaged over 1,000 bass per year, every year for the last quarter of a century!** That made the magic number 25,213 bass. It would be the third and final bass fishing milestone. Up until a few days before, I had not believed this goal was possible, and now I could hardly think of anything else. It could be done. It would be done!

I'll never be this close again. If I change my mind and decide to do it next year, it won't matter. The conditions will have changed. The window of opportunity will have closed, perhaps forever. If I'm going to make it happen, it must be now. One of my protégés, Kimberley Woods, informs me that *'Grace is God's unmerited favor.'* Whether earned or not, the God-given opportunity to catch 25,000 bass in 25 years now stood before me. I proactively decided to walk through that door while it remained ever so briefly open, with the clear understanding that this opportunity missed would be an opportunity lost, never to return.

Lesson: **Don't miss your opportunities—especially when they come up and smack you in the face.**

Lesson: It is often said that you get what you think about most of the time. This is true in all aspects of your life, whether you are looking for a better job, your dream house, or a perfect item of clothing. **If you still haven't found what you seek, don't give up. Instead, increase your commitment and intensity and you will accomplish your goal.**

Lesson: That annoying 39 bass total from the first year just might turn out to be the key to my success. Although I was always embarrassed at my poor initial showings, I could now see that it may have been a blessing in disguise. In fact, had the number been too high the first year, I might not have been able to better it with the amount of time left in the 2007 season. It seems that **man only second guesses the infinite wisdom of God's design when it does not immediately match his intended desires. Patience is a virtue, even if it requires your faith for 27 years.**

> *'To them that love God, all things*
> *work together unto good, to such*
> *as, according to His purpose.'*
> *- Romans 8:28*

Chapter 9: Is That All There Is?

> *'This is the way the world ends...*
> *not with a bang but a whimper.'*
> *- T. S. Eliot*

One of my protégés, Jasmine Grimm, told me that when she recently accomplished what she considered to be a monumental goal much sooner and easier than she had expected, she referred to it as an *'I shaved my legs for this!'* moment. Even as a man, I could relate to that feeling when the final bass was caught.

James Strickler, one of the property owners who gave me special permission to fish his private pond, asked me if I would catch the last bass (number 25,213) in his pond. How could I say 'no'? I told him that I expected to hit that milestone on September 11, 2007, and he was all set to be there for the 'big occasion.' However, with two days to go, I experienced some exceptionally productive fishing outings (106 bass combined). As a result, the moment of truth came a few days earlier than my prediction.

On day 40 of my 2007 bass season, 56 bass remained to be caught. Incredibly, the entire 39 bass (and then some) from my first season in 1981 had all been made up in one day! I then systematically hit each of my most productive ponds, racking up numbers and updating inquisitive property owners on my progress. There was no doubt in my mind that this would be the day I achieved my goal.

As I closed in on the last seven bass, I headed for Johnson Pond, my favorite fishing hole. While there I picked up my fiftieth lunker of the season (nineteen inches on the nose) with only three bass left to go, thus checking off yet another goal. And after the next bass was reeled in, I made a beeline for James Strickler's designated pond in search of bass number 25,213.

According to a quote by Franklin P. Jones, *'The trouble with being punctual is that nobody's there to appreciate it.'* Oh, how I could relate to that statement! On the way there, I called James Strickler to let him know I was on my way. James answered his cell phone but said he was not home. He was at a family reunion and could not leave. He told me to look around for his daughter when I got to his property and ask her to take a picture of *'the big event.'*

When I arrived, there was no one around. I called James back to say his daughter wasn't there. He said he would witness the bass by phone. I said I would call him back to confirm.

After only a single cast, using my favorite lure (the Heddon Tiny Crazy Crawler, grey mouse finish), I called James back and confirmed that at 4:15 PM on September 8, 2007, I had just caught my 25,213th bass, giving me an average of precisely 1,001 bass caught and released every year for the past 25 years-thus closing the chapter on the most demanding self-imposed commitment I had ever made. He congratulated me and a minute later I was standing there *alone.*

If a tree falls in the forest and there is no one there to hear it, does it make a sound? I believe a simple test, with the aid of a camcorder, will conclude that is does. Yet, there I was, all by myself thinking, 'It's really over.' It's not how I imagined. There were no television cameras, no reporters, no applause, and no celebration. Plutarch wrote in the *Life of Alexander* [the Great]: *'When Alexander saw the breadth of his domain, he wept for there were no more worlds to conquer.'* That may have been true for him, but I did not want it to be true for me.

With God as my only witness, I packed my gear, got in my car, and returned home hours earlier than my wife was used to seeing me. There was no big celebration there either, just a hug. It was as if I had said, 'I just weeded the yard,' only slightly *less* meaningful. You see, the time spent out there in pursuit of my dream was also time spent away from Kim.

I was grateful to my colleagues at Primary Staffing Services, who surprised me with a cake; and I kept the little plastic fisherman which now is displayed proudly atop my computer stand. This, along with my 25K BASS license plate publicity photo, some articles, my record keeping logs, and now this book are really the only tangible remnants from that accomplishment. Yet, they are more than enough because I wasn't seeking temporal rewards, but rather the knowledge and validation that anything can be accomplished with enough commitment, perseverance, discipline, time...*and plastic worms!*

When I first became a motivational speaker, I wanted to meet my role models—the most successful, world-famous speakers of the day. With very few exceptions, that has happened. I had my pictures taken with many of them. At some point, I intended to make a collage showing me standing with numerous legendary speakers.

But the more I knew of them, the less impressed I became. It wasn't because they weren't great speakers. It was because they did not turn out to be the people I thought they were. I don't take away their talent. I just discovered that when you look for human beings to emulate, you will still be selecting flawed role models, and you may be disappointed with what you find. As a result, I've learned to focus less on the individuals and more on their significant accomplishments.

Lesson: **What** I **did** should be less important to you than **the fact that** *it could be done.* That is what I would like you to take away from my accomplishments, along with the knowledge that **you too can realize your greatest destiny if you have faith in God, belief in yourself, and commit to your commitments. That may be all there is, but that is all you need to achieve true significance.**

Lesson: **Nothing worthwhile is ever accomplished without great personal sacrifice, dedication,** and harsh criticism. **Remember this when you are tempted to abandon your dreams because the path will most assuredly be wrought with adversity, challenges, and setbacks.**

Lesson: **Significance is in the eye of the beholder.** One person's milestone is another person's irritation. **Don't expect everyone to share your excitement over a personal accomplishment if it doesn't hold the same meaning for them.**

Lesson: It's often said that no man is a prophet in his own country. **Always know the real motivations behind the goals you pursue. Make sure they are significant to you, so that if you don't get positive reinforcement from those around you, it will not diminish your own enjoyment of your accomplishments.**

> *'Anglers have a way of romanticizing*
> *their battles with fish.'*
> *- Ernest Hemingway*

*For those of who enjoy numbers, bass fishing statistics, and goal-setting, I would like to make available to you the electronic versions of my bass fishing logs that I used to track my results, just like the ones featured at the end of this chapter. If you enjoy fishing, they may assist you in tracking your own results. If you don't fish, you may still gain some insights into how you can use similar tools to track and accomplish your goals. To get a FREE electronic version of *the Striving for Signifi-*

cance: Dave Romeo's electronic Bass Fishing tracking tools, just e-mail me at <u>daveromeo@embarqmail.com</u> and ask for 'SFS Bass Logs.'

Daily Bass Record Keeping Log: 2007

Day	Date	Daily Bass	YTD Bass	AVG. Bass Per Day
1	04/01/07	30	30	30.00
2	04/15/07	2	32	16.00
3	04/22/07	39	71	23.67
4	04/28/07	57	128	32.00
5	04/30/07	78	206	41.20
6	05/05/07	68	274	45.67
7	05/08/07	91	365	52.14
8	05/12/07	108	473	59.13
9	05/14/07	82	555	61.67
10	05/22/07	107	662	66.20
11	05/25/07	97	759	69.00
12	05/29/07	75	834	69.50
13	06/03/07	78	912	70.15
14	06/09/07	88	1,000	71.43
15	06/11/07	80	1,080	72.00
16	06/17/07	61	1,141	71.31
17	06/19/07	80	1,221	71.82
18	07/01/07	53	1,274	70.78
19	07/03/07	82	1,356	71.37
20	07/06/07	79	1,435	71.75
21	07/09/07	72	1,507	71.76
22	07/17/07	79	1,586	72.09
23	07/21/07	68	1,654	71.91
24	07/23/07	72	1,726	71.92
25	07/24/07	64	1,790	71.60
26	07/29/07	36	1,826	70.23

27	07/31/07		67	1,893	70.11
28	08/02/07		55	1,948	69.57
29	08/04/07		60	2,008	69.24
30	08/06/07		63	2,071	69.03
31	08/10/07		48	2,119	68.35
32	08/12/07		43	2,162	67.56
33	08/13/07		33	2,195	66.52
34	08/19/07		52	2,247	66.09
35	08/21/07		69	2,316	66.17
36	08/25/07		52	2,368	65.78
37	08/28/07		33	2,401	64.89
38	09/03/07		48	2,449	64.45
39	09/04/07		50	2,499	64.08
40	09/08/07		56	2,555	63.88
		Final	2,555		63.88

2007 Lunker Log for Bass 19 inches or larger

	Big Bass	Location	Date	Lure
1	19 4/8" LMB	Musser Pond	04/30/07	Plastic Worm
2	19 1/8" LMB	Musser Pond	05/05/07	Plastic Worm
3	19 6/8" LMB	Horace Jackson Pond	05/05/07	Crazy Crawler
4	19 6/8" LMB	Horace Jackson Pond	05/08/07	Plastic Worm
5	19 2/8" LMB	Johnson Pond	05/08/07	Plastic Worm
6	20 5/8" LMB	Musser Pond	05/14/07	Plastic Worm
7	20 0/8" LMB	Musser Pond	05/22/07	Plastic Worm
8	20 5/8" LMB	Musser Pond	05/25/07	Plastic Worm
9	19 1/8" LMB	Bruckhart Pond	05/28/07	Plastic Worm
10	19 1/0" LMB	Sweitzer Pond	06/03/07	Crazy Crawler
11	19 1/8" LMB	Bruckhart Pond	06/03/07	Plastic Worm
12	19 3/8" LMB	Strickler Pond	06/09/07	Plastic Worm
13	19 0/8" LMB	Johnson Pond	06/09/07	Plastic Worm
14	19 3/8" LMB	Terry Sweitzer Pond	06/11/07	Plastic Worm
15	19 3/8" LMB	Terry Sweitzer Pond	06/11/07	Plastic Worm
16	19 2/8" LMB	Terry Sweitzer Pond	06/19/07	Crazy Crawler
17	19 1/8" LMB	Terry Sweitzer Pond	06/19/07	Plastic Worm
18	20 1/8" LMB	Terry Sweitzer Pond	06/19/07	Plastic Worm
19	19 3/8" LMB	Terry Sweitzer Pond	06/19/07	Plastic Worm
20	19 1/8" LMB	Strickler Pond	06/19/07	Plastic Worm
21	19 1/8" LMB	Terry Sweitzer Pond	07/01/07	Plastic Worm
22	19 5/8" LMB	Terry Sweitzer Pond	07/01/07	Plastic Worm
23	19 4/8" LMB	Terry Sweitzer Pond	07/01/07	Plastic Worm
24	19 3/8" LMB	Terry Sweitzer Pond	07/01/07	Plastic Worm
25	19 2/8" LMB	Strickler Pond	07/01/07	Plastic Worm
26	19 0/8" LMB	Bruckhart Pond	07/03/07	Plastic Worm
27	20 0/8" LMB	Johnson Pond	07/03/07	Crazy Crawler
28	19 4/8" LMB	Johnson Pond	07/06/07	Crazy Crawler
29	20 2/8" LMB	Johnson Pond	07/06/07	Crazy Crawler

30	21 7/8" LMB	Johnson Pond	07/06/07	Plastic Worm
31	20 0/8" LMB	Johnson Pond	07/09/07	Plastic Worm
32	19 7/8" LMB	Terry Sweitzer Pond	07/17/07	Plastic Worm
33	19 4/8" LMB	Lower Knaub Pond	07/17/07	Plastic Worm
34	19 0/8" LMB	Smaller Wojtuzik Pond	07/21/07	Plastic Worm
35	20 2/8" LMB	Johnson Pond	07/21/07	Plastic Worm
36	19 1/8" LMB	Garber Pond	07/23/07	Plastic Worm
37	20 1/8" LMB	Johnson Pond	07/23/07	Plastic Worm
38	19 5/8" LMB	Johnson Pond	07/23/07	Plastic Worm
39	19 1/8" LMB	Johnson Pond	07/23/07	Plastic Worm
40	20 0/8" LMB	Sweitzer Pond	07/29/07	Plastic Worm
41	19 0/8" LMB	Maryann Reedy Pond	07/31/07	Plastic Worm
42	21 2/8" LMB	Garber Pond	08/06/07	Plastic Worm
43	19 0/8" LMB	Garber Pond	08/06/07	Plastic Worm
44	19 4/8" LMB	Johnson Pond	08/10/07	Plastic Worm
45	19 1/8" LMB	Musser Pond	08/13/07	Plastic Worm
46	20 0/8" LMB	Sweitzer Pond	08/19/07	Plastic Worm
47	19 1/8" LMB	Musser Pond	08/25/07	Plastic Worm
48	20 0/8" LMB	Musser Pond	08/25/07	Plastic Worm
49	19 0/8" LMB	Musser Pond	08/28/07	Spinner Bait
50	19 0/8" LMB	Johnson Pond	09/08/07	Plastic Worm

Career Bass Fishing Results			In order of Best Years		
1981	39	*	#1	1984	3,001
1982	147	*	#2	2007	2,555
1983	800	*	#3	2006	2,338
1984	3,001		#4	2005	1,563
1985	728	*	#5	2001	1,320
1986	502	*	#6	2000	1,296
1987	1,052	*	#7	1993	1,285
1988	347	*	#8	2004	1,281
1989	396	*	#9	2002	1,175
1990	259	*	#10	1994	1,151
1991	297	*	#11	1987	1,052
1992	524	*	#12	1999	826
1993	1,285	*	#13	1983	800
1994	1,151	*	#14	1985	728
1995	424	*	#15	2003	605
1996	448	*	#16	1998	550
1997	423	*	#17	1992	524
1998	550	*	#18	1986	502
1999	826	*	#19	1996	448
2000	1,296	*	#20	1995	424
2001	1,320	*	#21	1997	423
2002	1,175	*	#22	1989	396
2003	605	*	#23	1988	347
2004	1,281	*	#24	1991	297
2005	1,563	*	#25	1990	259
2006	2,338	*	#26	1982	147
2007	2,555		#27	1981	39

Current Year (next to the 1982 / 2,555 row)

Career: 25,332

	Total for the last 25 Years:	25,213
	Avg. Per Year:	1,001

119	Total Bass Kept (Lifetime)

25,213	Total Bass Released Alive (Lifetime)

0	**To go to reach 25,213 bass released alive (Lifetime)**
100.00%	**of goal to reach 25,213 bass released alive (Lifetime)**
22,658	**Total bass through 2006**
25,213	**Lifetime Goal**
-2,555	**bass remaining at the beginning of the 2007 season**
22,658	**Total bass through 2006**
-10.13%	**% of bass remaining at the beginning of 2007 season**
100.00%	**% of bass remaining caught during the 2007 season**
0.00	**years to go to reach 25,213 bass by 2007**

Chapter 10: Now What?

'I'm afraid of dying without
knowing why I really lived.'
- James Earl Jones as Alex Haley
(from 'Roots: The Next Generations')

With my final bass fishing goal complete, several questions still remained: Now what? What does this mean and what is its relevance in the whole scheme of things? It's all well and good to have achieved this goal, but what value will it bring to the lives of others?

Please don't think for a second that I had not considered this matter before now. On the contrary, it had been a topic of continuous contemplation for quite sometime. Personally, I experienced valuable lessons springing from my bass fishing pursuits almost on a daily basis. Yet, I knew that in order for them to be significant, I had to find a way for them to bring meaning to others, specifically the most important people in my life: my family, friends, and clients.

The challenge would then be to convert these experiences into teachable examples that would help people more easily accomplish their own dreams. As a teacher,

I know that the more realistic and vivid the lesson, the greater the likelihood that the educational seeds will germinate in the fertile minds of my students, whom I lovingly refer to as *'knowledge sponges.'*

One lesson I gleaned from my college experience came from an art history professor with whom I took three courses. She said, 'I don't care if you like a particular work of art or you don't. I do care that you can explain why. Do you like it for the richness of colors, for the romantic imagery, for the use of light, or for the political statement it makes? Do you dislike it because it is abstract or because it is disturbing in content or that it is out of proportion or that is makes you sad? This is what I expect of you: that you can clearly express how you feel and why.' I learned this lesson in 1976 and it has stayed with me to this day.

I once asked one of my best friends and clients, Elaine Bledsoe, why she came to so many of my seminars. Keep in mind that even though she has run a successful Tupperware franchise for the past 38 years, Elaine has been to more than 50 of my seminars. She said that she had been going to seminars for years where the speaker would say, 'This is *what* you do.' Elaine added that I was the first person who ever said, 'This is *why* you do it.' **This would become my trademark: to explain not only *what* to do but *why.***

As I said in the prologue, this is not a book about bass fishing. That is merely a metaphor. **This book is about *you*.** Actually, at this point, it is about us—you and me—for we are now connected and I believe it is my role to provide meaning, relevance, clarity, and focus to better negotiate the more challenging stretches along your earthly path. **I wish to help you discover the purpose of your life and inspire you to fulfill your destiny.** This should be very important to you. It is the goal we will accomplish in *Part 2*.

Lesson: **No one strives to be average.** My greatest fear in life has always been mediocrity—not counting for anything that matters. If by reading this book I can help you add meaning and fulfillment to your life, then we both will have escaped that dreaded fear of mine. Let us endeavor to do so now by going together in search of significance.

> *'The mass of men lead lives*
> *of quite desperation.'*
> *– Henry David Thoreau*

Part 2:
In Search of Significance

Learn all that is Learnable

*'To be what we are, and to become
what we are capable of becoming,
is the only end of life.'*
- Robert Louis Stevenson

*'Some fishermen, through a commitment to
lifetime learning, transform sport into art.'*
- Criswell Freeman

Chapter 11: Away from the Numbers

'And one man in his time
plays many parts...'
- William Shakespeare
(from 'As You Like it')

The time when numbers consumed my life has long since passed. I remember once writing in **Designing Your Destiny** that bass fishing is not what I do. It is who I am. Well, if that statement was true when I wrote it, it is no longer true today. Oh, don't get me wrong. I still use numbers in many aspects of my life—but no longer for bass fishing. I have not used my lap counter to record a bass in over a year and, as with **Part 1** of this book, that chapter of my life is now closed, but yet my journey is not over.

I have discovered a challenge I expect to be facing for some time to come from people who know me. When we first meet, they naturally ask, 'Have you been out fishing lately?' They are shocked and dismayed when I say, 'No. I'm not fishing anymore.' They continue, 'But you're not going to stop completely are you?' When I reply, 'Yes. Pretty much,' they are dumbfounded.

There is a story I read about how Charles Kettering, the inventor of the cash register, once bet his friend that if Kettering bought his friend a birdcage and hung it in his friend's home, sooner or later, the friend would wind up buying a bird. The friend accepted the wager.

After a while, Kettering's friend did buy a bird, because whenever someone would come to his house, the guest would look in the empty cage and ask, 'What happened to your bird?' He'd reply, 'I never had one.' Then the guest would respond with, 'Then why do you have a birdcage?' Eventually, it just became *easier* to buy the bird than go through that same routine.

I sympathize with Kettering's friend. The frequent inquires about fishing have gotten a bit tiresome, yet I don't mind that people ask. They are just being polite and sincere; and, besides, I spent over a quarter of a century reinforcing that expectation. However, it's not enough to induce me into resuming my previous passion.

When I told my business partner (who doesn't do a great deal of fishing but loves to hunt) that I was done bass fishing, he commented that the two of us do so many things for completely different reasons. I realize just how true that statement is. Let me attempt to explain how I look at activities and occupations.

When I was very young, my parents asked me if I wanted to join the Cub Scouts. I said 'Sure.' I went to every scout meeting. I participated in every activity (my favorite was making a balsa wood race car) and, like the other scouts, I pursued merit badges.

The next year, my parents asked me if I wanted to join the Boy Scouts. They were so surprised when I declined since I had enjoyed the Cub Scouts so much, but I felt it would be redundant and it had lost its appeal.

Have you ever re-invented yourself? I mean truly changed the way people see you and the way you see yourself. Let me walk you through the past four decades. In the 1970s, I used to eat, sleep, and drink anything that had to do with music. I played guitar. I wrote songs. I went on the radio as a music trivia expert. I went to 800 concerts in ten years (two hundred in 1978 alone). I was mesmerized at the ability of musicians to entertain and captivate such large groups of people through music. If you asked anyone who knew me back then, they would say, 'Dave Romeo? Sure, he's the guitar player' or 'the music trivia expert.'

It should be known that in my entire life, I have never taken any illegal drug or smoked a cigarette. My first legal-aged drink occurred when I was thirty-seven years old. (I was reading *The Holy Bible* in its entirety at the time and was interested in seeing how wine tasted since it was frequently referenced throughout *The Good Book*.) Alcoholic beverages do not appeal to me and if I never have another one in my life, I won't miss it.

The only reason I chose to share this very private information with you is so that you will understand that regardless of why anyone else may have gone to those concerts, my love of music was, and is, purely as an art form and a vehicle through which to reach and connect with other people in a positive way.

I played in a band that never lost a *Battle of the Bands* competition. My musical dream was to perform a concert where people would pay to hear my band perform my favorite songs in a high impact, entertaining show that would leave the audience screaming for more. I did that. It was an incredible feeling that I will never forget.

Not long after that show was over, I stopped playing in a band. As satisfying as the performance had been, I grew tired of being around people who did not share my values. Many of the musicians I played with were unreliable. It was not uncommon for our band to change drummers every week because we couldn't find one who could make two practices in a row. Many of the musicians I met took drugs and there was nothing I could do to stop it. A lot of the famous bands of the time were living in ways that I didn't wish to emulate. It saddened me to see how they squandered their incredible opportunities to reach people and be positive role models, and instead chose to destroy their lives with earthly excesses and their reputations with bad behavior. I was very turned off and stopped listening to their music. My path led elsewhere. It was time to move on.

If you asked anyone who knew me in the 1980s who Dave Romeo was, the answer you would most likely get was, 'He's that guy that is in the *Guinness Book of World Records* for bass fishing. He also runs Dave Romeo Bass Tournaments.'

I ran my tournament business for ten years from 1985 to 1994. It was so much fun. I had some contestants and volunteer supervisors who stayed with me for the entire time. What an incredible compliment! I also gained an enormous amount of experience about how to run a business (which has come in handy now that I work as a business coach for entrepreneurs). In fact, for the entire ten years, I had captured one hundred percent of the bass fishing tournament market on Long Island.

When I first began doing the fishing tournaments, I was single and living on Long Island. They were always held on Saturday mornings and ran from 6:00 AM to 12:00 Noon, so I could usually be home and all done by about 4:00 PM that same day.

After five years of running the tournaments by myself, I married Kim and the tournaments became a great deal more work to run because we lived in Pennsylvania. This meant we would have to pack on Thursday; leave on Friday; spend the entire weekend in New York; drive back on Sunday and take off Monday to tear down from the tournament, do the wash, square the sales records, and write up and mail out the tournament results. We were both working full-time jobs on top of this, so any vacation days we had would automatically be used to run the bass tournaments.

During the fishing tournaments, Kim would be on shore coordinating registrations and setting up the prizes for the winners. She'd sit patiently in the hot sun for hours, reading, occasionally listening for tournament updates (all the supervisors wore radio headsets so we could communicate with each other), and waiting for bathrooms breaks. PS: Many of the places where we held

the tournaments had no bathrooms, just big bushes—
and plenty of mosquitoes!

One time Kim was bitten two hundred times even though she had just bought new mosquito repellent and applied it generously. I remember because I counted the bites as I applied the pain relief lotion to her fair skin. To this day, I still cannot believe all of the sacrifices my wife endured to indulge me because of that business. It must have been love.

When I told Kim that after ten years I would be ready to stop running the fishing tournaments, she didn't believe that I was serious (although I'm sure she hoped that I was). Yet, that is exactly what happened.

I had learned all that was learnable about running my bass fishing tournament business. And, like performing a concert, I loved promoting events where people could come and have some of the most unforgettable times of their lives. This knowledge would not be wasted, but rather transformed through a different vehicle in yet another career that was somewhere still some years away.

In 1990, I moved to Lancaster County, Pennsylvania in the heart of Amish Country. I became a staffing recruiter (also known as a headhunter). I started off very slowly; but by the time I was done seven years later, I had become the number one recruiter for the printing industry in America.

If you asked anyone who knew me in the 1990s, they would surely say, 'Dave Romeo is ***the recruiter*** for the printing industry.' I set sales records, gross profit records, and even net profit records for my company, and continued to break my own personal records. In addition, prepping job applicants was great practice for the job coach I would later become. Getting employers to give my job candidates a try helped me master my ability to communicate, influence, and negotiate.

Many times I would have to paint word pictures so people could see themselves succeeding in a job before they would accept a position. I did the same with my client contacts. I gave them the confidence to give my job applicants a chance. These valuable skills would become the essential skills I needed to effectively perform as both a seminar presenter and a results coach later in my life.

At the peak of my success as a headhunter, the company I worked for was sold to another company. As with the musicians I played with twenty years earlier, we didn't share the same values. Also, I was getting requests from clients to perform services other than recruiting. They wanted me to teach customer service training to their staff. They hired me to evaluate their salespeople. I was getting many requests for consulting work ***even though I wasn't a consultant!***

I realized, at the time, that even though I was successful in my role as a recruiter, I had pretty much done all I could do. In fact, I had outgrown the position. Has that ever happened to you? It was the same job I held and loved for seven years, but it seemed to have lost its challenge and, consequently, its appeal. Once again, it was time to move on to something new.

Today, if you ask anyone who knows me, 'Who is Dave Romeo?' they will most likely say that I am either a motivational speaker or a results coach. It seems so clear now that this would be the logical next step in my career. All of my previous positions and passions have prepared me to entertain, enlighten, and inspire my clients. And that is the point: ***nothing is wasted.*** We generally use what we have learned at some point in time, but not always in the way we expected.

Lesson: **You do not want to be forever defined or limited by your job description. Furthermore, each role you play in life prepares you, in part, for the next role.** Think of your career as a series of acting roles. An actor wants to master his part and become the absolute best he can be. But many actors fear becoming so closely identified with a role that they will become typecast and unable to experience the joy of stretching their talents into new and more challenging roles. Don't do the same with your life. According to Napoleon Hill in his book, *'Think and Grow Rich,'* almost all of the successful men he interviewed made their most significant accomplishments well after they turned forty years of age. **If you want to achieve something great, keep learning from each and every stage of your personal and professional development.** Remember, as the song says, *'The best is yet to come.'*

Lesson: **Reinvention is healthy. As committed as I am to finishing what I start, after accomplishing goals, it's all right to move on to something new.**

With this in mind, my plan is to show you how to take the lessons of your life and apply them in ways that will greatly enhance your future. Once you've absorbed this chapter's lesson, let's start practicing the art of gleaning from the past in order to enrich the present.

> *'Don't let your past dictate who you are,*
> *but let it be a part of who you will become.'*
> *- Nick Portokalos*
> *(from 'My Big Fat Greek Wedding')*

Chapter 12: Nobody's Fault but Mine

'If it's to be, it's up to me.'
- Anonymous

Believe it or not, not everything I've learned in recent years has occurred while bass fishing. For example, I recently made a very humbling discovery about myself *in my garage*. I caught myself instantly seeking someone to blame for something that was frustrating me.

I went to put on my cordless headphones, which I wear every morning when I exercise. The batteries had gone dead, so I went back upstairs to get some new ones. I then went out to the garage to put the old ones in a recycling bag. The bag was in a large cardboard box which holds car supplies like anti-freeze, transmission fluid, and ice scrapers. However, when I went to drop the batteries into the recycling bag, I missed. Now I had to scrounge around under a large load of bags of empty soda cans. These cans are there because we save them for two of our closest friends who turn them in for money. They are saving up the money for their children's college tuition.

I was so annoyed as I felt around blindly, searching with my one free hand to locate the tiny AAA batteries in the cluttered cardboard box. Of course, this was completely my friends' fault, because the only reason the box was full of bags of cans in the first place is because we haven't seen them recently. If *they* had only called us to get together, I would have given our friends the four bags of cans and I wouldn't now be fumbling around looking for those cursed batteries. Instead, I'd be on my way to the office as I had planned. So you see, *it was really my friend's fault* for not calling more often to initiate getting together with us.

Why am I sharing this story with you? It's because I want you to ask yourself if this sounds familiar to you. Am I describing the way you rationalize away your own culpability and seek out others on which to place blame when things go wrong?

Sadly, I realized that this was exactly how I was approaching almost anything that didn't go my way, especially if it was due to my own actions (or inactions).

This revelation forced me to take a long hard look at myself and my actions. I didn't like what I saw. I realized that I really needed to find a way to instantly take personal ownership for my own actions and behavior.

So, how exactly does one go about doing this? The first thing I had to do was make a mental promise to accept that I am the person most likely to be responsible for the actions and consequences I experience.

The most empowering lesson that came out of this revelation was that **I had the ability to immediately** change the things about myself and my behavior that I did not like. That's what free will is all about. I had to accept that even if I didn't cause my negative circumstances, I was the person best suited to improving the situation.

Lesson: How about you? **Do you find that you are always making excuses for your own lack of prosperity, success, or happiness? You can change this today if you want to, and it won't cost you a red cent to do it!**

I do want to make an important point. As human beings, we tend to see the world in black and white. It's all or nothing for us. We're either winners or losers, successes or failures. Well, let me throw another consideration into the mix. We're all imperfect human beings and we will lose and fail at least as often as we win and succeed. There is no other way to get where you are going. I make this point because I see too many well-intentioned people beat themselves up when they experience a setback. They also allow it to destroy their self-image and self-confidence.

Let me assure you up front that **you *are* going to experience setbacks and disappointments. Accept this fact right now and you won't be derailed when they occur.** The good news is that you are not alone. Any successful human being you can think of had to suffer adversities and challenges before they became successful.

Lesson: Do not label yourself as a loser when you don't succeed. **Part of taking responsibility for your** own actions is accepting that you are not perfect and that failure isn't fatal. **Understand that experiencing life's lessons are necessary for you to achieve significance.** As the master of optimism, Zig Ziglar reminds us, *'Failure is an event, not a person.'* These setbacks are the stepping stones which will allow you to grow stronger and handle greater accomplishments.

Don't expect to wake up one day following this plan and never encounter a negative thought for the rest of your life. If you tend to blame others for your own actions, you're unlikely to undo the habit in one day. It probably took you many years to develop a negative attitude and it will take some time for you to develop the positive habit of instantly taking personal responsibility. As Denis Waitley says, *'You cannot break a habit. You can only replace a habit.'*

What I can tell you is that you will enjoy many benefits by following this mindset. You will be a lot happier and you'll become a much better companion. You'll also become more popular with your loved ones, your friends, and your clients.

What I could have said to myself when I dropped those batteries was, 'Next time I'll just take the bags of cans off the box before I drop the batteries into the recycling bag. This way, I'll know that they are exactly where I want them to end up.' No blame, no excuses. Just clarity of purpose and a clear statement of fact. If I take this action, I'll get my desired outcome.

You will most likely also continue to experience lapses of negativity from time to time, if not on an ongoing basis. **Don't allow yourself to become victimized by your surrounding circumstances. Make a commitment to take responsibility for your actions and the consequences that follow.** To paraphrase Mahatma Gandhi, it's time for both of us to be the change we wish to see in the world.

> *'Life is difficult. It is a great truth*
> *because once we truly see this truth, we*
> *transcend it. Once we truly understand*
> *that life is difficult—then life is no longer*
> *difficult...once it is accepted, the fact*
> *that life is difficult no longer matters.'*
> *– M. Scott Peck*
> *(from 'The Road Less Traveled')*

Chapter 13: The Waiting Room

'If we're all alone, then we're
altogether in that too.'
- Elizabeth Kennedy
(in 'P.S. - I Love You')

It's funny how life goes in cycles sometimes. Did you ever notice how all of a sudden it seems like your friends are all getting married or maybe having babies? I suppose some of that is merely age-related. Many common events in our lives are triggered as we reach certain ages.

About a year before I closed in on my bass fishing goal, several of my dearest friends and clients went through the same sad experience—the death of their fathers. All of them were Christians. All of them were women about the same age and each of them had a deep-seated appreciation, love, and respect for their dads.

Being a results coach allowed me the great privilege to get close to these women and to comfort them in their time of grief. Not having any children of my own, I was truly humbled at the outward demonstrations of pure, unadulterated admiration these women held for their fathers. I can still remember one woman expressing herself so genuinely through her uncontrollable tears a few weeks before she lost her father. She said, 'I just love my dad and I want him with me always.' There just were no adequate words to console someone going through that grieving life passage.

In an attempt to comfort my friends, I have shared with them a metaphor I use when someone is about to face being separated from parents or loved ones who depart this world before us. The metaphor I share is called, ***'the waiting room.'***

If you've ever gone to the doctor or the dentist, then you know what a waiting room is. It's where you must spend some of your time before you eventually get to where you originally intended—with the doctor. Your duration in the waiting room will not be the same length of time as everyone else there. In fact, some people will already be there ahead of you and other people will arrive after you get there. Occasionally, someone gets there after you and goes in ahead of you. It is merely a fact of life, timing, and unknown circumstances.

While you are there, you can decide how you to spend your time. You may read a magazine, perhaps watch television or sit quietly and wait.

You may decide to only talk with someone you know who may have accompanied you there, or you might reach out and spend some time talking with other people whose time in the waiting room overlaps with yours. Your situation is at least one thing you both share in common. You may not be as close to the people that you meet because of coincidental timing and circumstances, yet your interactions with them may be surprisingly rewarding and enjoyable and may help make the time you spend in the waiting room more pleasant and meaningful—perhaps even *significant.*

Now, let's compare the waiting room metaphor with our temporal life. While you are here on earth, you can decide how to spend your time. You may decide to keep to yourself and wait, or just interact with a small group of close, personal friends, or perhaps stay only with your family. After a while, you may still only talk with people you know or you might become more outgoing and look forward to spending time meeting new and interesting people whose lives happen to overlap with yours. Your circumstance is at least one thing you have in common. You may or may not get as close to these people as you are to your family, but you may discover that their inclusions in your life may be even more rewarding and meaningful and may help you spend your time on the earth in a more fulfilling way.

My dad once told me how sad he is sometimes to be separated from his parents, grandparents, aunts, uncles, and sister who have all passed away. However, he added that it would only be about another twenty years or so before they would all be reunited. In the mind of God, twenty years is an instant. It will come and go; and, depending on how you have lived your life, it may seem like a lifetime or a blur.

When I say waiting room, please don't get the mistaken impression I am suggesting that you sit around waiting to die. Nothing could be further from the truth.

What I mean is, in the great scheme of things, **our only purpose for being on this earth is to earn the opportunity to someday achieve heaven. With that as the prize, all other accomplishments pale in comparison.**

This is not meant as sad news or depressing news but is, in fact, great news. If you think about it, in one sense, *the waiting room* should really be *a living room*. You see, so many people worry about their jobs, about money, about being liked, about failing, and about rejection. However, once you put eternity in perspective, you realize how none of these things are worth a moment's concern.

As a public speaker, you continually put yourself in a position to fall flat on your face and be judged or criticized for your presentation. Yet when you realize, 'Hey, this is merely a diversion from my true purpose,' it allows you to let all feelings of self-doubt melt off you and evaporate. Allow this awareness to free you from fear and enjoy the wonders and possibilities that life holds in store for you.

The amazing power of a book is that, in a way, it extends your reach in the waiting room. You can write a book and even after your death, you may still have the ability to connect with someone born years after you've gone. It is your connection. It creates overlaps with others that will allow you to accompany someone in a future era while they wait.

Someone once made the observation that the only people who are really remembered long after their deaths are writers, artists, and entertainers. Let's see if this claim holds up.

I realize one could make the case that leaders (both positive and negative) are often remembered long after others of their generations have been forgotten. I'm referring to people like Noah, David, Herod, Jesus Christ, Julius Caesar, Joan of Arc, Napoleon, Hitler, and Winston Churchill. But for argument sake, we'll exclude leaders.

By writers, lets include poets like Sophocles, John Milton, Robert Burns, and Henry Wadsworth Longfellow; playwrights like William Shakespeare and George Bernard Shaw; authors like Charles Dickens and Jane Austen; and people like Saint Paul the Apostle and Saint Thomas More. It could also include composers like Mozart, Gilbert and Sullivan, George Gershwin, and Irving Berlin. By artists, we might include sculptors like Michelangelo; painters like Rembrandt van Rijn, Vincent van Gogh, and Pablo Picasso. By entertainers, we could include actors like Clark Gable, John Wayne, and Sir Laurence Olivier; comics like Abbott and Costello, Jackie Gleason, and Rodney Dangerfield; musicians like Ray Charles and Jim Croce; and singers like Elvis Presley, Karen Carpenter, and Frank Sinatra. Although none of these people are still alive, they have the ability to reach us and connect with us. Their works live on after them and serve as pleasant diversions for those of us still here on earth.

As I say to my dear clients and friends who have lost a loved one (and to you as well, my reader, if this too is your situation), have peace in knowing that in the blink of an eye, you will be reacquainted with them once again and it will be forever. And, in the meantime, I'll just keep you company for a little while here in the waiting room.

Lesson: **There are some things in life that are within your control and some things that are beyond your control. Learn to focus on the things you can influence and release the rest to God. You are not privileged to know how much time you have to live, but you do have control as to what you do with the time you are given. There are people in your life who have much to contribute to your well-being. You can also choose how much of yourself you are willing to offer others.** You may not even realize just how much significance you have in other people's lives as we shall see in the next chapter.

> *'It's not where you start that*
> *counts—it's where you end up.'*
> *- Dave Romeo*

Chapter 14: You're My Best Friend

'I never met a man I didn't like.'
- Will Rogers

Growing up in the small town of East Meadow, New York on Long Island, I didn't have a lot of friends in my neighborhood because most of the time I went to private schools. My parents were friends with another East Meadow couple and so, by default, I sort of became friends with their son, Christopher (Chris) who was a couple of years younger than me.

Chris was one of the few kids in my town who also went to the same schools as me, so we were on the same buses and attended some of the same functions. Chris and I didn't have many common interests. Come to think of it, I don't think I ever remember him talking about fishing. However, we did both share a deep love of music, although not always *the same music.* Growing up in New York during the Seventies and early Eighties was a great place to be because there were always different musical acts coming to town.

I remember calling the local concert hotlines almost every week to find out what musical acts would be coming to our area. I specifically remember one time finding out that a band I really liked was coming to Radio City Music Hall, but the show was already sold out. When I told Chris about it, he said, 'Oh yeah, I heard they were coming, but I wasn't interested in seeing them.' I said, 'Then why didn't you tell me when you found out?' He said, 'Because I didn't want to go.' I said, 'Well I did want to go. I tell you about every concert I hear of, whether I want to go or not, just so you know who's coming. Why didn't you just tell me so I could get tickets?' Again he said, 'I just wasn't interested in going.'

I was really upset with Chris after that instance. He struggled to understand why this bothered me so much, but I don't think he ever really got it. This behavior was typical of Chris and he often frustrated me. By the way, Chris didn't have many friends of his own and most of my friends didn't like him very much either. I can't say that I was surprised.

One day, we went to New York City to see a concert at the Palladium. Along with us were my brother Jack and another friend. By the time we found a parking space around the block from the building, Chris was as sick as a dog. You see, earlier that same day, Chris had taken the last of his final exams and when he was done, he went drinking with some of his classmates. This was very uncharacteristic of Chris. Neither one of us drank alcohol, and he certainly wasn't used to hard liquor.

Shortly after we parked, Chris became so sick that he threw up. I didn't know what to do for him. He couldn't easily stand up on his own and I had two other people with me who wanted to go in to see the concert. Chris said, 'I can't go in. I'm just going to sleep here in the car until the concert is over.' I felt bad about leaving him in the car, but I didn't know what else to do. I told Chris that we would come right out as soon as the concert was over and take him home.

Reassured, but still a little queasy, he said, 'Thanks, Dave. You're my best friend.' I was so surprised by his words. I thought to myself, 'I'm your ***best*** friend? I can hardly stand the sight of you! How could I be your best friend?' Of course I didn't actually say that. But I thought to myself, 'I would ***never*** treat my best friend the way he treated me. And if I ***was*** his best friend, ***this*** is how he would treat me?'

But as I reflected on this later, I wondered if maybe I ***was*** his best friend. As I already said, he really didn't have a lot of friends and maybe I was the closest person to him. It made me see him differently and, hopefully, I was more forgiving of Chris' idiosyncrasies after that night. The Lord knows I have more than enough of my own to go around.

I've tried to take that memory from 1980 and use it as a reminder to approach people with kindness, patience, understanding, and love. Trust me, I haven't mastered this yet, but I'm much more conscious of it as a result of that incident than I had been before. Every year, I strive to add some great new people to my life—people that I can truly consider my friends.

Lately, I've had more and more of my clients, both men and women, break down and cry in their coaching sessions. One of my clients confessed that I was the only man she would ever allow to see her cry. I regard it as a very high compliment that she trusted me enough to let her guard down.

I challenge you to make it your mission to make someone in your life feel as if he or she has a best friend in you, even if that person isn't yours. Life can get overwhelming at times for people and sometimes they may not always verbalize what they are going through. Allow them to find solace and compassion in your company.

Lesson: **Everyone you know could use a best friend. And it's OK to have more than one.** I've been blessed with two, and they are also both each other's best friend. It's like a perfect triangle of comradery. Still, if my other friends consider me their best friend, that's an honor that I cherish.

Lesson: **Someone need not be *your* best friend for you to be *his or hers*. It will not detract from you for someone else to feel that way about you, but it may do that person more good than you'll ever know.**

Lesson: **Never underestimate the significance of the role you play in someone else's life.** Only the other person can truly know that, and your friendship may be the best thing that person has going for him or her. **Use your compassion abundantly and have charity to those you touch in their time of need.**

> *'You are not the solution to everyone's problem, but you are the solution to someone's problem.'*
> *– Mike Murdock*

Chapter 15: God Bless Karen Johnson

'Blessed are the peacemakers:
for they shall be called the children of God.'
- Matthew 5:9

One of the best things about living in Lancaster County, Pennsylvania is the abundance of farms and, with them, farm ponds. This is where most of my bass fishing has taken place over the past thirteen years. I learned how important it was to ask permission to fish these private bodies of water. By **earning the right** to fish them, I gained nearly exclusive access to some of the best largemouth bass fishing in the United States. This was accomplished by continually demonstrating respect for the farmers and their families who owned them.

Farming is true toil and I found it ironic that almost all of the farmers who gave me permission to fish on their property **never went fishing at all!** They had no time. Sometimes I would fish these farm ponds and go for years at a time without even seeing the landowners because they were always engaged in laborious work.

I imagine that some people might look down on people who work with their hands in the dirt for long hours every day (except Sundays); but I have nothing but admiration for their pureness of purpose and their tireless dedication to bringing the rest of us the freshest produce, meat, and dairy products at a moment's notice when we go to the supermarket.

Some people might think that farmers don't accomplish anything really significant because of the work they do. In fact, those same people might even consider their own work insignificant. That's because they sometimes lose sight of just how valuable a contribution they are actually making.

I've met many people through the years who felt like they were working in dead-end jobs that were in some way demeaning. They didn't feel appreciated in their jobs or that what they were doing was really that important. Yet, if that were true, then one of the most incredible individuals I've ever had the privilege of working with would have probably gone unnoticed by most people because of her natural low-key humility.

Karen Johnson was one of the most unassuming, kindly people you would ever want to meet. Karen became the third point of a perfect triangle: a three-person team (along with my fellow recruiter, good friend, and protégé, Bernadette Hill, and myself) which was dedicated to staffing printing industry employees for our clients' companies. Our team went on to lead our entire organization with the highest team gross profits and net profits. I later learned that the accountants in our company's corporate office would hold their collective breath in anticipation each week, waiting to hear how our printing team did because we would ultimately determine whether or not they would be getting their profit-sharing bonuses.

When Karen joined our team she served as our administrative assistant. From the very beginning, she made it clear that she was not interested in selling or in making placements. I was not sure that a three-person team could be profitable with only two revenue-generating team members, but that was before I witnessed Karen Johnson's uncommon work ethic.

If you've ever seen the television show *M*A*S*H** you might remember the character Radar O'Reilly. As the story goes, he earned his nickname because he had the innate ability to anticipate things that were about to happen or things someone might need. Karen shared this same intrinsic gift and used it to an extraordinary degree for the benefit of our clients and our team.

As the inimitable Yogi Berra is credited with saying, *'You can observe a lot by watching.'* That was one of Karen's secrets to success. When she first joined our team, Karen made a point of not only learning *her job*, but also *our jobs*. As recruiters, Bernadette and I were responsible for getting new and existing clients to give us job orders to fill and then filling those positions with job candidates whom we would personally interview, pre-qualify, prepare, and send out on interviews to meet with our clients.

Yet, before Karen joined our team, Bernadette and I would waste a great percentage of our valuable sales time trying to collect our employees' completed and signed time slips (many of which were late every single week), and answering questions about how much longer it would be before our temporary-to-hire candidates could become employees of our client companies. Keep in mind that we could not bill our clients without those signed time slips, so that meant we would not be paid.

Without ever being asked, Karen proactively made a checklist of every employee who was currently out working on assignments for us. Then she would check off every time slip that had already been turned in to our office by our Monday morning processing deadline. She then called the candidates who had not yet turned in their time slips to retrieve those as well. Without fail, Karen was collecting all of the completed time slips on time so Bernadette and I could spend more of our time filling additional job orders.

In addition, Karen built a computer file which kept track of how many hours each candidate had worked so she could tell our clients when our assigned candidates could become their employees. Karen updated the file on a weekly basis using the hours recorded on the time slips she collected from our candidates. Both clients and candidates could now get the up-to-date information directly from Karen faster than they could from the recruiters, who now had *even more time* to fill job orders. **Karen was turning her administrative position into a profit center before our very eyes, *without ever making a sale!***

Since Karen generally answered our phone first, you might expect her to say something like, 'Dave, Sharon Mitzell is on the phone for you.' But with Karen, it was usually more like this: If I was on the phone, Karen would get up, go to the resume file, pull a particular resume and wait until I was finished with my call. Then she would say, 'Sharon Mitzell from York Graphics is on the phone. She needs a second shift, four-color, Heidelberg press operator who can start work on Monday.' Then, handing me the resume, she'd continue, 'This candidate just called in a few minutes ago. He just lost his job and is available for work immediately. He lives in York and said he is open to working a second-shift position.'

Keep in mind that Karen did not do these tasks because someone asked her to do them. She simply took the time to learn our business and then went on a never-ending quest to find ways to design out the flaws in our system and add value wherever she could.

One of the most memorable stories which epitomized *the Karen Johnson standard of excellence* happened after she had been working on our team for a while. I had a big project in mind, so I asked Karen if she could come over so I could explain it to her. She said she was already in the middle of a project but that she would come to me as soon as she completed her current task.

I thought it was odd that Karen did not come back to me that same day, and I initially figured she either forgot about my request (which was completely out of character for Karen) or, more likely, that she was still working on her other project.

On the afternoon of the following day, without me asking her a second time, Karen came over and said, 'OK, Dave, what did you need?' I started to explain my request to her. I said, 'As you know, we have a file folder for every printing company in Central Pennsylvania. Could you please make a set of file folders for every printing company in the Scranton area?' She then said, 'Well I figured you would want that so that's what I've been doing.' The point is that Karen never slacked off, even after she had proven her value. She couldn't because that was not who she was.

I cannot leave out three additional qualities that made it a joy to work on such a team. First, there was Karen's pleasant disposition. She was such a delight to work with and she treated all of our clients, candidates, and co-workers to her warm and sparkling personality. Simply stated, *if you knew Karen, you loved Karen.*

Second, there was Karen's natural ability to practice tact and diplomacy in every situation. If she ever had a bad day, you wouldn't know it. She used diplomacy, patience, and kindness to create a calming effect on all those around her. As anyone who has worked in the staffing industry can tell you, it can be an extremely tense and pressure-filled environment. There is a constant demand to produce results faster than your competition (whom, in many cases, may be your own clients, as they are also desperately trying to save money by filling their own internal job openings). Yet, through the craziness, Karen's example of genuine humility, compassion, and pure likeability helped us to regain our focus on serving our customers.

There have been many presidents, CEOs, and VIPs that I've met and served over the years and many of them

I've forgotten. I've worked with some great co-workers in my day, yet I cannot remember all of their names. But I will never forget Karen Johnson. She was my moral compass, my benchmark for always acting honorably when serving my customers. I never wanted to diminish one iota of the respect she showed me.

Third, the level of mutual respect on that three-way team was unmatched by any other team I have ever participated in or observed. The three of us got along so well because we each shared the common goal of developing mastery in our field and treating all those we served with legendary customer service. Also, we each recognized and valued just how integral each one of us was to the shared success and magic of our team.

Sadly, not all corporate decision makers could appreciate the true value of every employee, not even ours. Years later, our company was sold to another business entity and Karen was let go. The short-sightedness of that decision was the clearest indication that it was also time for me to go.

Incidentally, all three members of the printing team left within a few months of each other. There was no point in staying. The significance of Karen's firing was that we now realized that our employer was unable to recognize just how significant a role she played in the printing team's success. However, her value was much more evident to our clients, many of whom also left when we did.*

Within two years, the company stopped placing printing people, laid off the replacement recruiters, and closed their Lancaster County office, which had housed the printing team. That decision cost them millions of dollars in lost revenues, never to be seen again. In fact, that company no longer exists. What a waste. Bad judgment and poor decisions like this one led to its downfall.

Lesson: **Significance is not always measured in dollars and cents.** Sometimes it takes more than just business savvy to be successful. You also need to be people smart. **Karen Johnson represents the silent heroes that upper management often cannot see, but who are the personification of the organization to its top producers and to its customers.**

Lesson: There are no insignificant jobs or positions. The significance does not lie in the title but rather in our commitment to the duties. If you will approach what you do with a passion to be great, you will either transform the position or you will be transformed by the experience. You will decide where your future lies. You will also attract the notice of those in authority who recognize the significance of someone who is driven to be the best. You will become a positive influence on those around you, some of whom you probably never thought could be reached. And you will become a role model to others who also strive for significance.

Lesson: **Never underestimate the power of your personality. Karen was one of the most likeable and well-respected people in our organization and with our customers.** For example, one year, one of our most demanding clients came to our office bearing gifts of appreciation for all the help we had given him to staff his pressroom. He brought personally-selected individual gifts for all three of us, including Karen. And while she never made a placement for this client, he knew just how integral she was to our team's performance, and he was right. Ask yourself, 'Have you ever seen a client (who never even met your administrative assistant or even came to your office), select, purchase, and personally deliver gifts of appreciation to her?' In many cases, you would probably be amazed if your clients even knew her name. Yet, in Karen's case, she simply made herself unforgettable.

Regardless of your position, job, or area of responsibility, I challenge you to follow Karen Johnson's example. By doing so, you will be blessing all those around you with significance.

> *'Don't wish for a better job. Do a better*
> *job and you'll have a better job.'*
> *- Charlie 'Tremendous' Jones*

* By the way, this story is continued in much greater detail in my book, *'Nice Guys Finish First! — How to be a Winner Without Losing Your Integrity.'* If you are interested in reading more about this story, you can conveniently purchase any of my books by calling Primary Seminars & Coaching at (717) 569-9700 or by emailing me at <u>daveromeo@embarqmail.com</u>.

Chapter 16: Who was Kristin Otto?

'In the future everyone will be
world-famous for 15 minutes.'
- Andy Warhol

Have you ever heard of Kristin Otto? If you said 'no,' that would be a shame. In 1988, this East German athlete became the first woman to win six gold medals in the Olympics for swimming. Think about the amount of personal commitment, drive, and sacrifice required to win **even one** gold medal, **let alone six!** So why don't we know who Kristen Otto is? At the time of this writing that was just a mere twenty-one years ago! I hate to admit it, but the only reason I've heard of Kristin Otto is because her last name was the answer in a recent New York Times Sunday crossword puzzle. Talk about a humbling revelation.

Did you know that Don Larsen pitched a perfect game? Can you imagine how hard that would be to do? What an incredible milestone for any ball player. It's what every pitcher must dream of. Not only that, he pitched that perfect game for the New York Yankees in game 5 of the 1956 World Series! To this date, it still ranks as the ***only*** perfect game to ever be pitched in post season play. ***How incredible!*** That has to be as good as it can ever get for a pitcher. Now tell me the truth. Did you ever even hear of Don Larsen? No? How can that be? The man should be a legend, and yet you are unlikely to encounter anyone today who would remember his great feat. Why do I know it? Again, it was an answer in another New York Times crossword puzzle.

How ironic that a man with such an unbelievable accomplishment should be relegated to nothing more that bit of trivia fifty-three years later. Yet, **thus is the nature of fame. It is indeed fleeting and we should remember this when we experience any degree of it. It does not insure significance.**

Lesson: **When seeking significance in your own life, do not make the mistake of pursuing one single achievement or obtaining an object. Either may bring you temporary satisfaction, but neither will insure long-lasting significance or even an inclusion as a *Jeopardy* clue.**

It was never my intent to get to the point where I could rest on whatever laurels catching 25,000 bass might muster. (Whatever they are, for the most part, still remain to be seen.) What one does get from accomplishing a personal milestone is another layer of confidence and the personal satisfaction of realizing one's reliability. It better prepares you to face your next challenge with greater focus.

Keep in mind that it won't necessarily prevent other people, external events, or circumstances from occasionally distracting you from your achievements. It may, however, lessen their affect on you. Remember, as my framed lithograph from the *Successories* product catalog correctly claims, *'In the battle between the river and rock, the river always wins...not through strength, but through persistence.'*

So what about you? For what will you be most re-membered? What have you done that will have people talking about you years after you've left this earth? Well, before you start scrambling to locate some dusty old bowling trophies, moth-eaten varsity jacket, or badly battered beauty contest tiara, let me spare you a trip to the attic.

Perhaps what will serve as your greatest accomplish-ment will be the ability to live a life full of mistakes but free of scandal. There is more merit in staying married to the girl (or boy) next door than making the newspapers over your messy celebrity divorce. You don't need to fill arenas to make a difference, just fill a child with wonder and possibility by reading a classic bedtime story. As the master observer of human nature, Will Rogers once chal-lenged, *'Try to live your life so that you wouldn't be afraid to sell the family parrot to the town gossip.'*

Lesson: **You will avoid a great deal of personal disappointment if you keep a healthy perspective on your own self-worth.** Accomplishments, no matter how noble or momentous, will eventually be forgotten. **Focus instead on the person you are becoming and whom you may be inspiring when evaluating your own contributions.**

'I long to accomplish great and noble tasks, but it is my chief duty to accomplish humble tasks as though they were great and noble. The world is moved along, not only by the mighty shoves of its heroes, but also by the aggregate of the tiny pushes of each honest worker.'
- Helen Keller

Part 3:
Putting it Together

TEACH ALL THAT IS TEACHABLE

'And He saith to them: Come ye after me,
and I will make you to be fishers of men.'
- Matthew 4:19

''Tis not all of fishing to fish.'
- Izaak Walton

Chapter 17: I Like Your Style

'Vision is the art of seeing things invisible.'
– Jonathan Swift

Do you have a style? Yves St. Laurent once said, *'Fashion fades but style is eternal.'* That may be true, but did you ever wonder where style comes from? It must be extremely rewarding to invent a way to captivate others with your talent.

I've always been fascinated by people who had the ability to visualize something great before it exists. Let's take a composer, for example. If you live in the United States, you are almost certain to be familiar with the song *'Happy Birthday to You.'* This song was copyrighted in 1935 and credits Preston Ware Orem and Mrs. R. R. Forman as the authors. It is such a simple tune. It is considered to be the most frequently sung song in the English language, which certainly qualifies it as significant. Now, imagine that you came up with that melody first. Do you know how much money you would earn? Copyright laws require a royalty fee of up to $10,000 for its use in a movie or television program, giving it an estimated value of around $2,000,000 per year. Talk about making your talent *pay off!*

Yet, the song was supposedly a variation of an existing song entitled *'Good Morning to You'* which is credited to kindergarten school-teaching sisters, Patty and Mildred Hill, for the song's melody in 1893. By the way, the only difference between the melody in *'Good Morning to You'* and *'Happy Birthday to You'* is one split note to accommodate the extra syllable in the word *'happy.'* In other words, had the very first word in the latter song contained only one syllable instead of two, it would have been considered the same melody as the former song and there would be no royalties paid when *'Happy Birthday to You'* is used in a movie or on television. *We're talking about the significance caused by a single syllable!*

Items like the microwave ovens, cell phones, e-mail, and GPS (Global Positioning Systems) are all incredible inventions that many people now consider indispensable. Yet, someone had to think them up before they existed. I've always marveled at how people create something from nothing. That is true vision.

Years ago, Kim and I traveled with our friends, the Peters, to New England. One of the first stops we made was to the Barnum Museum in Bridgeport, Connecticut.

What I remember best about our visit was a film that was running which featured the actor Burt Lancaster playing P.T. Barnum. That was eleven years ago so I don't remember the exact words, but at the end of the film loop, Burt Lancaster turns towards the camera and says something to the effect of, **'Genius is the art of seeing what already exists, but is invisible to everyone else. That's what I did. I invented the audience. I invented you.'** What an incredible concept! Let me explain why this was such a powerful message for me.

What did you want to be when you grew up? Did you have something very specific in mind for yourself? I think most people have asked themselves these questions from time to time. I repeatedly hear many of my adult coaching clients over fifty years of age still trying to decide what they want to be when they grow up.

For me, it started when I was about twelve years old. I thought for sure that I would be a singer in a band. As I've previously mentioned, much of time during my college years was spent watching the most successful bands of the day perform live. One of the benefits of growing up near New York City was easy access to all forms of entertainment. No matter where a band was from, or how popular they were, they always wanted to play in **The Big Apple.**

Some of the performers I saw between 1973 and 1981 included: Aerosmith; Alice Cooper; The Allman Brothers Band; America; The B-52s; Bachman Turner Overdrive; Bad Company; The Beach Boys; Jeff Beck; Pat Benatar; Chuck Berry; Blondie; Blood, Sweat & Tears; Boston; David Bowie; Jack Bruce; Eric Carmen; The Cars; The Charlie Daniels Band; Cheap Trick; Eric Clapton; Roy Clark; The Clash; Crosby, Stills, Nash & Young; Deep Purple; Rick Derringer; Devo; Bob Dylan; The Edgar

Winter Group; Dave Edmunds; ELO; Emerson, Lake and Palmer; Fleetwood Mac; Foghat; Foreigner; Peter Frampton; The Go-Go's; Lionel Hampton; Heart; The Jam; The Jefferson Starship; Jethro Tull; Billy Joel; Elton John; Journey; Kansas; The Kinks; The Knack; Led Zeppelin; Paul McCartney and Wings; Meatloaf; Eddie Money; The Monkees; The Moody Blues; The Outlaws; Pink Floyd; The Pretenders; Queen; The Ramones; REO Speedwagon; Robin Trower; The Rolling Stones; Rush; Santana; Paul Simon; Frank Sinatra; Slade; Squeeze; The Steve Miller Band; Rod Stewart; Supertramp; The Sweet; The Talking Heads; Ten Years After; Thin Lizzy; George Thorogood and the Destroyers; Tina Turner; Uriah Heep; Van Halen; Muddy Waters; The Who; Johnny Winter; Gary Wright; Yes; and ZZ Top.

As you can see, it was quite a diverse group. Also keep in mind that I didn't just go to see these artists once, but as often as I could. I saw some of them as many as twenty times. You see, I was completely mesmerized by how these different performers could use the same few musical notes, played on different instruments, in differing orders, and create such an endless combination of music.

When I wasn't going to concerts, I was going to see the local bands performing in nightclubs. I just couldn't get enough exposure to music. After all, I was going to be the singer in a band. As an afterthought, I decided I should learn how to play guitar. That way I could learn how to write music and my own songs. It wasn't that important that I be a really great guitar player because, as I said, I was going to be a singer. The singer gets to entertain and connect with people in a very special and unique way. You can hear two different singers perform the exact same song and each one will put his or her own individual style to it. Yes, that's what I'll do. I'll be an entertaining front-man who can play guitar, write my own music, and sing.

There were, of course, a few minor glitches in my plan. The first one was that I couldn't sing. Ironically, I was about the only person who didn't know that I couldn't sing. Not That I wasn't told—my dad *repeatedly* tried to bring this fact to my attention. But then, after all, he was *my father!* What did *he* know about singing? He'd never even seen Led Zeppelin or The Rolling Stones. He was just saying that because he didn't want me to become a singer.

Do you want to know how I found out that I couldn't sing? One day I was taping myself playing one of my own songs on the guitar so I could practice playing lead guitar on top of the arrangement. The tape recorder was running and I was strumming. I couldn't wait to play it back and hear this *'great musical masterpiece'* and add my magnificent harmonic accompaniment to the rhythm track. But something was terribly wrong with what I heard. Along with the *adequate* guitar playing, there was this painfully disturbing utterance coming from my tape player.

It was so bad, it was painful to listen to and it was *ruining* the music. I didn't know what to make of it at first. Perhaps my *used* tape recorder (which I had purchased at a flea market) was damaged. And then, the sad realization finally hit me. *It was my voice!* Without even realizing that I was doing it, I had been singing along to the guitar track. *'That's what I sound like?'* I exclaimed. *'That sounds terrible!'* It sounded like Lou Reed. Now, some people might like Lou Reed, but I didn't and I certainly didn't want to sound like *him!*

I was crestfallen. I had no idea that I really couldn't sing, but even I couldn't bear to hear that wretched sound. As you might imagine, this put a *'minor'* crimp in my singing career plans. How was I supposed to be a singer when I really couldn't sing? (By the way, this was, of course, many years before Milli Vanilli, Brittany Spears, and Ashley Simpson all proved that musical talent was not required to be a singer.)

Oh well, they say, *'Where there's a will, there's a way.'* So I decided that if I couldn't sing, at least I could become a great guitar player. I'd seen so many great guitar players who completely amazed me with their talent. They too could captivate audiences with their musical prowess. Yes, that's what I'll do. I'll become a great guitar player. It's a good thing I knew how to play a guitar. In fact, I decided to go to college *as a music major.*

Again, I ran into another minor glitch when I went to the school. *They required an audition!* Let's just say that it was another humbling experience, one that closely rivaled my Lou Reed sound-alike moment. For future reference, if you decide to take up music lessons, it's a good idea to learn from someone *who actually knows* how to play the instrument. I was self-taught.

(**Remember, I also *taught* myself how to sing**. You get the idea.)

While I was used to just strumming along with songs I heard on the radio and learning the chords to songs by watching local cover bands performing in nightclubs, the college admissions committee expected me to know how to read classical music in order to perform in their orchestra. I had not realized that this particular school *discriminated against students who lacked any actual musical ability.* In any case, they would not accept me into their music program unless I learned how to first play classical guitar. There's *always* a catch!

I did take lessons for a few years at the *world-renowned* East Meadow Conservatory of Music. (*No doubt you've heard of it*.) Don't be fooled by the name. The owners probably would have opened up a pizza parlor instead of a music studio if they had had a little more space. Anyway, the music lessons didn't really help. I wasn't interested in playing classical guitar and I never became very good at it. I didn't really mind that much because at least I could play music I liked in local bands while I finished my college education…*as an English major.*

One thing I'll say for my father, while he didn't like my singing voice, he told me that I had an excellent speaking voice. He suggested that I go into the field of broadcasting. 'How ridiculous,' I thought. 'I can't sing and I'm not a very good guitar player. *How am I supposed to make a living just using my voice? I mean, people don't pay you just to talk, do they?*'

Let's fast forward to 1993. I'll never forget the first time I ever heard a motivational speaker. I was working as a headhunter at the time. It was a good job, but I was still searching for something I could do that would be unique and entertaining. The vice president of the company told us that we were all going to the Yorktowne Hotel, but he didn't say why.

When we arrived at the historic downtown hotel, we marched into a room that had been reserved (for some still unknown purpose) for our organization. There was a television set in the large meeting room. The vice president popped in a videocassette of a live presentation by world-class business presenter and author Tom Peters. I was instantly captivated by what I heard. I didn't really know much about Tom Peters at the time, other than he had co-written the best-selling book, ***In Search of Excellence***. I hadn't read the book. In fact, I don't think I had ever read a business book in my life up until that time, but I was passionate about great customer service. And so were all the people listening to him. ***Who knew?***

When Tom Peters began presenting, it was like nothing I had ever seen or heard before. He was speaking to a packed house, but he wasn't a musician or a singer. He wasn't particularly attractive nor was he in exceptionally great shape. He was in his forties and he was dressed in a business suit. He didn't tell jokes, but he got laughs and applause. The people in his audience hung on his every word. So what did he do? He talked. ***He told stories.*** He ranted and complained about things he didn't like and what we needed to do about them to make things better.

And best of all, he spotlighted great organizations that did things right. *It was incredible. It was uplifting—it was entertaining, enlightening, and inspiring!*

From that moment on, I knew what I wanted to do...*I wanted to be Tom Peters.* How incredible to have your words mean something. This man was living my dream. He was the center stage star without being a great singer or musician or dancer or comedian; and yet he was treated like a rock star by business people. I thought to myself, '**Maybe I *can* make a living telling stories.**'

I just loved his style. Unfortunately for me, **I didn't *have* a style.** Everything I knew, I learned from Tom Peters. My style was his style, but the problem was, *I wasn't Tom Peters.*

I finally had the opportunity to meet Tom Peters a few years later in Harrisburg, Pennsylvania. He signed copies of his books for me and even posed for a photo with me. I told him how he had inspired me and that I used to want to be him. But then I realized that it would be cheating because he was such an original. He ***developed*** his style. He did not ***copy*** it. And so I told him, 'I don't want to ***be you.*** I want to be ***better than you.***' And Tom Peters, my role model leaned in, smiled at me, and said quietly, 'Now, you've got it.'

Not long after I had originally heard of Tom Peters, I had a similar initial reaction when I first saw motivational speaker Tony Robbins live on stage in Philadelphia. Wow! I can still remember that day as if it were yesterday. He was unbelievable. There were about sixteen thousand people in attendance. Tony Robbins is 6' 7" tall. He has a commanding presence. He made quite a striking pose as he wore a white dress shirt and suspenders. At one point, he jumped off the stage of the Spectrum Arena and then ran up the steps, down the aisles, and all around the building, high-fiving people as he passed them. I had never seen anyone whip a crowd into such a frenzy without a guitar in his hands. He was truly amazing. 'Maybe,' I considered, 'I should be Tony Robbins!'

I mentioned to one of my great friends and clients, Karen Fink, that I wanted to be just like Tony Robbins and she helped me to finally see things a little more clearly. She said, 'We don't need you to be just like Tony Robbins. We need you to be in between Tony Robbins and us so we can actually reach out and speak directly with you.' This was something I had never considered because I didn't know anyone who was doing it.

This happened to me over and over again as I discovered other speakers and authors I really admired. Ken Blanchard's writing and speaking style was pure genius in its simplicity and clarity. John Maxwell combined tasteful, anecdotal humor with inspirational, faith-based lessons.

The more different speakers I heard, the more they began to influence me and, with time, something magical happened...***I developed my own style.*** If you look carefully, you'll see that it is a combination of Tom Peters' passion, Ken Blanchard's simplicity, Tony Robbins' enthusiasm, and John Maxwell's inspiration, blended with some Dale Carnegie for his understanding of human nature and Zig Ziglar's positive motivation. You'll see influences of Johnny Carson's perfect timing and wide appeal, Jerry Seinfeld's comedic observations, and Jay Leno's brilliant wit. There are also some of Emeril Lagasse's methodic organization and Rachel Ray's charisma, confidence, and perfect delivery thrown in for good measure. (***Why did we have to start watching The Food Network?***)

What makes my style different from all of these great influences is that it is overlaid with my love and knowledge of music, references to goal-setting, record keeping, and, of course, life's lessons learned while bass fishing. All these elements, coupled with accessibility, helped me finally create a style I could be proud to call my own.

Lesson: Perhaps **that is the true definition of style. It is combining all of the most positive influences in your life to form something familiar, but slightly different and, therefore, totally unique.** And, as style is developed it becomes, to some, even more appealing than the original influences. In fact, many of my 'knowledge sponges' are unfamiliar with my original influencers. I take great delight in introducing them to the brilliant minds they might not otherwise have known.

Lesson: **Discover your own unique style.** Don't waste time copying others. Take the best of all you find and put it together in a new combination that will become unmistakably your own.

Lesson: **Style is not so much invented from scratch as it is 'tweaked' from that which already exists.** Find what you like and make it better. Make it significant. Make it yours.

As we continue to grow in our pursuit of significance, we must come to terms with what can be accomplished by combining what is already known and adding to it our own personal flair to create something truly original, unique, and, mostly importantly, achievable.

> *'You don't need to be helped any longer.*
> *You've always had the power*
> *to go back to Kansas.'*
> *- Glinda*
> *(from 'The Wizard of Oz')*

Chapter 18: You are a Great Human Being

'Perfection is not the goal.
The pursuit of perfection is the goal.'
- Dave Romeo

Do you consider yourself to be a great human being? I'll bet you are and don't even realize it. How can I make that claim without even meeting you? It's easy. Let's break it down. You are great if you recognize that you have God-given talents that can help you to improve your life and the lives of those around you. Perhaps you haven't yet **mastered** your talents to their fullest potential, but with time you still can.

When it comes to being a human being, by our very nature, we are flawed. We make mistakes, we err in our judgment, and we let ourselves and others down. We cannot live a perfect life. At best, we will make tiny errors that will have minor consequences to ourselves and the people around us. But beware that **a life marked by only tiny errors is quite likely to be only remembered for tiny accomplishments, assuming it is remembered at all. As with most things in life, it's a trade off.**

Our goal, therefore, should be to become great human beings. That is, we need to rise above our flawed human nature and have the courage to strive for greatness and significance in the face of our own limitations.

Do you have that courage? *I* know that you do, but *you* must realize it too. *Your destiny depends on it.* Today and every day after, you may be called on to test your courage and your judgment.

Sometimes we allow our setbacks to damage our self-esteem. When this happens, we tend to lose sight of our great qualities. We find excuses to discount our own self-worth. It is even worse if this opinion is reinforced by the people around us. The more we value their opinion, the more painful their words can sting. **But as Eleanor Roosevelt once observed, *'No one can make you feel inferior without your consent.'***

This is a good place for me to pass along to you ***'The Four S. W.'s: Some Will. Some Won't. So What? Someone's Waiting.'*** Remember that no one else's opinion of you is as important as your opinion of yourself. **You are the person that God intended you to be and you must live up to your potential. 'So how do I do this?' you may ask. Let's put a plan in place.**

First, you must **acknowledge that you have God-given talents**. To deny this would be foolish. But if, as I said, your self-esteem has been damaged, you may have trouble believing that you have talent. If this is true about you, you can reconcile that your talents are God's handiwork and you need not concern yourself about being worthy of them. Since God is perfect and He gave them to you, realize that He wanted you to have these talents. About this point, there can be no mistake.

Next, you must accept that since you have these talents, it would be a terrible waste not to use them. Unused talent is like throwing away unused food. Neither serves a purpose and neither should be wasted.

One year, for Christmas, one of my mentors, Sharon Mitzell, gave me three blank journals. I thought this was ironic at the time because she knew how much I loved to read, and yet she gave me three books consisting totally of blank pages! But Sharon always carried around journals with her to write her to-do lists, record new concepts and ideas, and add reminders to send to specific people at a later time. Sharon is one of the most sought-after human resource specialists I know, so I decided to put her gifts to good use.

What I discovered was that during any given day, I am hit with great ideas that come and go in an instant. (*As I grow older, they've been going much quicker than they have been coming*). In addition, people are always telling me great quotes that they have heard, many of which I use in my seminars, coaching sessions, and—you guessed it—in my books.

Sharon's journals have been the perfect place for me to record all those valuable gems in one place so they do not get away from me and I can find them when I go to put my thoughts down on paper.

My point is, just having been given the journals (or gifts) was not enough. I could have squandered Sharon's gifts if I didn't find uses for those journals, and I would have been the one who missed out. The same is true about talent. **It is not enough just to possess talent. We either develop it or we waste it.**

Lesson: **Our next step is to master our talents. Whatever your talents may be, you have the ability to become an expert if you are willing to hone and develop them. Let us learn to accept and cherish our talents as we would any precious gifts. We must show our appreciation for our talents by embracing them and using them to their fullest potential.**

> *'I'm not where I'm supposed to be. I'm not where I want to be.*
> *But I'm not what I used to be. I haven't learned how to arrive.*
> *I've just learned how to keep on going.'*
> *– John Maxwell*

Chapter 19:
Spinner Baits, Plastic Worms, and Discipline

**'Many of life's failures are men who
did not realize how close they were
to success when they gave up.'**
- Thomas Edison

I was driving to work one morning after some television coverage regarding my 25,000 bass pursuit. As I was stopped at a light, a motorist who had noticed my license plate (that's right: the *'confounded'* one), pulled up along-side of me. He rolled down his window and said, 'How do you catch so many bass?' I wasn't sure how to adequately answer his question in the five seconds before the traffic began moving again. I quickly gave him the best answer I could think of which was, 'Spinner baits, plastic worms, and discipline.' But since you have given me a little more time to express my thoughts, please allow me to elaborate on this concept. And if you do run into that inquisitive motorist, maybe you can pass this information along to him for me.

One of the advantages of catching so many bass in a relatively short period of time is that you pick up on patterns and trends. Many of these patterns and trends hold up when you translate them to other aspects of life. Let me give you an example. Between 2006 and 2007, I caught 4,891 largemouth bass in eighty-one days of fishing. More than 4,700 of these were caught on either spinner baits or plastic worms.

Spinner baits are great because you can cast them a great distance and cover a vast expanse of water in a relatively short period of time. When bass hit spinner baits, most of the time they are instantly hooked in the mouth. They are easily landed and released with minimal downtime. To give you some perspective on just how effective these lures can be, consider this: the most bass I've ever caught in two hours was 63—all of them on spinner baits. One day in 2007, I caught fifty bass on spinner baits without losing a single lure. No downtime!

Now, you might think, 'Why wouldn't you just fish with spinner baits all the time?' The reason is that spinner baits don't work in all conditions. They work best in open water. If you run them through underwater vegetation, they'll usually get covered in weeds and become useless until they are cleaned off, which causes downtime.

Spinner baits generally don't work well on bright sunny days or in very deep water. They do work well when there is a breeze and the water's surface is choppy. Bass are usually more skittish in bright sunlight. They try to avoid being visible to birds of prey. Therefore, spinner baits are better suited to fishing when the sky is overcast with clouds. In other words, the conditions need to be right to use spinner baits.

Plastic worms, on the other hand, will work extremely well in even the thickest weeds, whether the water's surface is flat or rough. Sunlight does not prevent bass from striking a plastic worm, provided you are willing to invest the extra time to use them. You see, fishing with a plastic worm is closer to hunting than fishing. You are targeting one specific fish at a time. In many cases, you have already spotted the bass before you cast to it. It requires much more time and patience to catch a bass with a plastic worm. Just because a bass strikes a plastic worm doesn't mean it's hooked. It can still spit out the lure. While the worm is in the bass' mouth, the hook may not be. Also, bass are far more likely to swallow the hook when you use a plastic worm than a spinner bait. When this happens, you must cut the line so the fish will survive, put on a new hook and a new worm. This creates even more downtime.

The point is that both plastic worms and spinner baits are excellent lures for catching bass. However, if you were to use only one or the other, you would not catch as many bass as you could if you use a combination of both. The key to successful bass fishing is knowing when to use one or the other. It all comes down to discipline. There were many times when spinner baits were working great for hours and then the action just stopped dead. No matter what I did, I could not catch another bass on a spinner bait. I would get spoiled using the easier lures. Even though switching to plastic worms would take longer, I knew that they would be infinitely more productive.

I tell you this story because the spinner bait verses plastic worms example is such a perfect metaphor for life. If you only use one method to do anything, you will probably fall short of your goal. For example, I sell seminar seats for a living. If I e-mail a full year's seminar schedule to a customer, I will first highlight my personally, handpicked recommendations for that individual. This can be time-consuming because some of my customers have been coming for years and may have taken many of my seminars already.

However, using this method has become as productive for filling seminar seats as fishing with plastic worms has for catching boatloads of bass. The average sales call using this method generates an average of fourteen seminar sales. It sure is more effective than the old method I used to use. That consisted of me calling about forty to sixty people and asking each one of them if they wanted to see the seminar flyer for an upcoming seminar. If they said 'yes,' I would e-mail them the flyer and call them back the next day. This method generated about one sale for every fourteen people I called. Unfortunately, as soon as that seminar passed, I would have to start that process all over again to sell the next seminar.

One of the mistakes I made when I changed over to selling an entire year of seminars in one call was that I didn't go back after the customers that only bought one or two seminars a year and who usually didn't make a commitment until thirty days before the actual event. I eventually realized my error, and it was lucky for me that I did. Had I not gone back and made those time-consuming slower individual calls, **I would not have been able sell out my entire year of seminars *by July!***

There is a terrible old joke that I once heard about a young bull and an old bull looking down over a pasture. The young bull says, 'Wow! Look at all those cows down there. Why don't we run down and get one?' The older, wiser bull says to the impatient youngster, 'I've got a better idea. Why don't we walk down and get them all?' You can probably glean the point of this metaphor. This is exactly how I caught so many bass. It was a constant willingness to practice good judgment and employ the discipline demanded of the conditions. Abraham Maslow once commented, 'It is tempting, if the only tool you have is a hammer, to treat everything as if it were a nail.' In life, we miss many opportunities because of our reluctance to try something new or different, even when we know it will be better.

Lesson: **Whatever goal you set for yourself, understand that you will need to make sure you do everything necessary to bring it about, not just the easy steps or the tasks you enjoy doing the most.**

Lesson: **Bass fishing, like leadership, is a continuous exercise of judgment and decision-making.** Neither the spinner baits nor the plastic worms were as instrumental to catching all those bass as was the discipline to stop using one and the willingness to switch over from the comfortable choice to the other lure when necessary. Procrastination is the friend of evil. Remember this when you are charged with making decisions that will affect not only your outcome, but also that of the people you serve.

'From discipline comes freedom.'
– Dave Romeo

Chapter 20: One Moment in Time

'If people concentrated on the really
important things in life, there'd
be a shortage of fishing poles.'
- Doug Larson

I'd like to tell you the story about the photograph on the cover of this book. The person who took that photo was Phil Garber. I only met Mr. Garber once before he snapped that picture. But it is very likely that I might never have met him at all. Here's how it came about.

About three years ago, Susan Kauffman (***my guardian angel***), who works at the Lancaster County Chamber of Commerce, introduced me to Rhonda Campbell. Rhonda was a frequent speaker for the Chamber of Commerce. The two us had never met, but we both knew Susan because she was the Chamber's contact person for all the outside presenters.

Rhonda called me one day to introduce herself as a referral from Susan Kauffman. I knew that if Susan was referring Rhonda to me, she had to be a terrific person. I was right. We met for lunch and instantly became fast friends. Rhonda even agreed to do a few speak-

ing engagements for my company, Primary Seminars &
Coaching, and they were very well received.

About a year ago, Rhonda introduced me to Rodney
Garber, a nice young man from whom Rhonda had
purchased a water softener. Rodney lived one town away
from me and, for some reason, Rhonda thought the two
of us should meet. I called Rodney and we met for lunch
on a Friday in June. It was one of only two times I have
ever met him.

As we talked and got better acquainted, the subject
of bass fishing came up. We discussed my 25,000 bass
pursuit and how difficult it was to find productive new
private ponds to fish in the area. Rodney mentioned
that his family built a pond about eight years earlier
on their extensive commercial farm property in Mount
Joy, Pennsylvania (where I used to live from 1990 until
1997). The Garbers wanted their pond to provide a place
for people and organizations to take kids fishing. The
pond had been stocked with largemouth bass seven years
earlier. Rodney said I was welcome to fish there.

Let me explain why this pond became so valuable.
First, it was close by. Sometimes I would find a great
pond that was over an hour away. It may have been productive, but I would have to trade off hours of valuable
fishing time driving back and forth. Having another
private pond this close by meant it could be easily fished
as a stop-over pond on the way to another body of water.
The more ponds in close proximity to each other, the
higher my daily average would climb.

Second, it was a private pond. That meant it would not be heavily fished. Since it had been stocked, I already knew it held bass. More importantly, it had been stocked seven years ago. As many serious bass anglers know, a new pond is usually the most productive in the seventh year after stocking. By this time, there could be some very sizable bass swimming around in Garber Pond.

Third, it was an enormous advantage to have permission before I learned of the pond. Even though I had lived in that town, it was unlikely that I would have ever found this pond on my own. It was located on a back road and, at the time I went searching for it, completely hidden from view by an extensive cornfield.

I couldn't contain myself. I left the restaurant and drove straight to the pond just to make certain I could find it. It was beautiful and fairly secluded. I couldn't wait to come back the very next day and give it a try.

When I did return, I caught bass there from my very first cast. In fact, I believe they hit on every lure I tried. Most of the bass I caught that day were not very large, but I did watch a lunker-sized bass follow my lure right up to my feet.

While I was there, Rodney stopped by to see how I was doing. We only spoke for a short time because he was with one of his friends who was getting married later that same day. While I was speaking with both of these gentlemen, someone else drove up in a car, parked, and walked up to Rodney. As he introduced us, I discovered the stranger was none other than Rodney's father, Phil Garber. Phil and I spoke briefly so I could tell him what

I was doing. After a short visit, he reiterated Rodney's permission to fish their pond, wished me luck, and was on his way.

With only twenty-seven fishing trips separating me from my goal, that pond became a strategic goldmine. Even if it didn't produce many big bass, it was easy to access, fish for a short while, and then move on to a number of other private ponds in the area.

As I sensed that I was drawing ever nearer to my goal, one thought kept popping into my mind: I'm going to need a promotional photograph to accompany the press release when I catch the final bass. Experience has taught me not to expect the last bass to be the most photogenic. I was catching plenty of sizable bass along the way, but there were very few people present to photograph the big ones.

On August 6, 2007, the day before I turned forty-nine years old and fifty-eight days after meeting Phil Garber, I landed a beautiful 21 ¼ inch largemouth bass that weighed approximately six pounds. It was perfect! I knew when I saw it that this was the fish that would be forever associated with my goal. The only problem was, there was not another soul in sight.

Fortunately, there were several signs on the property notifying people that they had to first obtain permission before fishing that pond by calling the phone number listed on the sign. Even though I already had permission, I dialed the number in hopes that someone there could help me.

Without knowing to whom I was speaking, someone at Garber Farms answered the phone. I explained that I was down at the pond and had just landed a six-pound bass. I said that I was in need of someone who could take a picture of me and the lunker. The man on the other end of the phone must have asked around to find out what to do. When he started speaking with me again, he told me to sit tight and that someone would be down in about five minutes.

I patiently waited, remembering that I didn't have my digital camera with me. I did have a thirty-five-mm waterproof camera, but I'd trusted it less and less lately with important photos. ***'Why didn't I tell the person on the phone that I needed a camera too?'*** I reflected. I suppose I thought it would be too presumptuous to do that. After all, whoever was coming down to help was already taking time away from their job to lend me a hand.

Right on cue, an automobile appeared from behind the wall of corn stalks that surrounded the pond. The car barreled down the dusty gravel and dirt road. It was Phil Garber, Rodney's father and the owner of Garber Farms and all the property on which I was fishing. He remembered me vaguely from our only other meeting nearly two months earlier. God Bless Phil: he came equipped with a very nice digital camera, without even being asked.

My last few years of fishing had provided me with plenty of time to envision what the perfect shot should look like. It would obviously have me holding up the sizable largemouth bass, mouth open in the forefront, with my trusty Bass Pro Shops Bionic Blade fishing rod propped up against my knee in front of the tranquil, blue water from the accommodating pond in the background. I also knew that the picture would look just like any one of the hundreds of other photographs I'd had taken over the years if it wasn't for one additional inclusion-it had to have that confounded license plate proclaiming '25K BASS' somewhere in that shot.

Please keep in mind that while I had this going on in my head, Mr. Garber had never given this photo a moment's consideration before my phone call. Yet he patiently waited as I attempted to recreate that image I had been storing in my mind for so long.

I had to move my light blue Saturn L200 closer to the pond to line up the shot and crouch down very unnaturally against the back bumper of my car in order to fit everything into the camera frame. The rain held off long enough to take about a half dozen photos. I naturally thanked Phil Garber for graciously coming to my rescue in my time of need and asked him if he would be kind enough to e-mail me downloaded attachments of those photos. He assured me he would. But when? I couldn't possibly impose on him any more than I already had, so I figured I would just wait patiently and if I didn't hear from him after a week, I would call to thank him once again and then *tactfully* remind him about sending me the pictures. But my fears turned out to be unfounded-a few hours after Phil Garber left me, I stopped in my office at work. The photos were already waiting for me when I arrived.

When I reviewed the finished products, I saw that there were a couple of dandy photographs from which to choose. I liked the way my chartreuse-colored Dave Romeo Bass Tournaments fishing cap covered *most* of the grey hair that, incidentally, wasn't present when I initially started this quest (*thanks a lot, Mom!*). To my delight, my tape measure and bass counter could be seen hanging from my sun-bleached Plano shirt that had somehow held up for over two decades of fishing excursions.

With only 32 days remaining before the final bass was caught and released, bass number 24,734 would become the most visible and memorable bass of my accomplishment, thanks to Phil Garber, a man till this day, I've only met four times.

Lesson: **No one enters your life by accident. Don't prejudge a person's importance or contribution. People you meet a handful of times, or even just once, have the ability to change your life.**

Lesson: **The reverse is also true. Don't underestimate how big a contribution you can make in someone else's life. Do as much good for as many people as you can possibly touch. Insist on being significant wherever and whenever you can.**

Lesson: **Networking is a valuable practice, whether you wish to increase your sales or discover new places to go.** What would have happened if Susan Kauffman hadn't referred me to Rhonda Campbell (who, by the way, did not even know Rodney's family lived one town away from me or had a pond)? What if Rhonda hadn't introduced me to Rodney Garber? And what if the one day I fished Garber Pond while Rodney was there, he didn't introduce me to his father Phil, who just happened to stop by while I was there? Don't leave it to chance. **Be proactive and never miss an opportunity to connect with a potential new friend.**

> *'One should not depend on an*
> *unbroken series of fortunate events.'*
> *– Senator Justin*
> *(from 'Roots')*

Chapter 21: I Don't Want to Miss a Thing

'Go and find your smile.'
- Barbara Robbins
(from 'City Slickers')

Did you ever notice how often it is that we learn to find contentment in the simplest settings? Recently, I have taken a much greater interest in my yard, specifically my lawn. I've noticed some bare spots. They are not new, but I never really paid them much attention before now. They were just something I hardly noticed in a quick glance between fishing trips. But now that my fishing trips are a thing of the past, my skills of observation are seeking out new areas of interest that had previously been overlooked.

I must admit, when I first contemplated life after bass fishing, I was afraid I might be bored out of my mind. What exactly was I going to do with all that newfound time on my hands? What I have since discovered is that my sense of adventure still longs to be satisfied, but that it need not be from something as all-encompassing as my bass fishing opus.

One thing I did know for sure was that I would not look to replace that time with anything else that would keep me away from my wife Kim. She has been my silent hero for so long, supporting my bass fishing pursuits even though it meant staying out all day away from her companionship. It was long overdue for me to reposition her as the center of my world and make her my priority.

Yet, there had to be a way to feed my desire to know more and to discover more about life. Thus far, my attention has turned toward becoming the steward of my own property. Never have I found my own yard so full of wonder. Would you believe I now take great joy in weeding? I must admit that it has become easier with the aid of some foam kneeling cushions that I converted from a pair of gardening pads I once taped together and used to protect my automobile from being damaged by my car-top bass boat.

When I was in sixth grade, my teacher, Mr. Tobin, challenged his class to take a one-hundred-inch hike in our backyards-to get down on the ground and start looking very closely at everything that goes on right under our noses. I must admit that while I had not forgotten about his suggestion, I never actually took him up on it until recently. But I can't believe how interesting it has turned out to be. I could get lost for hours at a time, ***voluntarily,*** in the microenvironment of our juniper- and black-eyed Susan covered hill and marvel at the way different plant life springs forth despite all kinds of barriers. It would seem that **not all lessons need be learned**

while bass fishing; and that itself is also a lesson worth learning-you can find so much in everyday life that will reveal to you the most amazing discoveries. I can now tell you that I discovered that fact *without ever leaving my yard!*

Mike Ferro and Bob Kandratavich are two of my top coaching clients. Both of them work for Tomlinson Bomberger, a lawn care and landscaping company in Lancaster, Pennsylvania. Tomlinson Bomberger has long been a sponsor of my seminars and one of my largest clients. I've had the privilege of presenting seminars to the entire organization on numerous occasions.

Being that company's customer also has given me some great advantages. For starters, it has allowed me direct access to two top professional landscaping authorities. They are an endless source of valuable and accurate information to me in my new-found intrigue with flora. In addition, over the years the lawn care technicians created an enormous amount of free time for me by taking care of my yard, which I then converted into productive bass fishing time.

But now that I am no longer distracted by wondering which pond will produce the most bass under the current weather conditions, I am finally paying attention to the yard I was so anxious to race away from on my way to the next fishing outing.

I asked Mike Ferro about how to fill in some of the bare spots in my yard. I thought it would give me something to do. I followed his instructions; yet, it still seemed to take forever to see the results. As I continued my daily watering, I began to notice several mounds of dirt lying precisely where I had planted some new grass seed. I couldn't figure out from where they had come. We have no outside pets and no children. **'*Who was throwing dirt bombs on my lawn?*'** I wondered.

One day, I reached down and picked up one of the dirt mounds and realized what had happened. There were about fifty newly-sprouting blades of grass underneath the impediment. They had all banded together to move the dirt and sprout their way to sunlight.

I was captivated at the sight-the wonder of a few blades of grass, strong enough to push forth a solid mound of dirt and break free to grow. How magnificent to see such an accomplishment made by some the planet's smallest living things! **'*Having seen these seedlings perform this incredible miracle,*'** I thought to myself, **'*can we be expected to do less?*'**

The point is, **you can find a miracle in your own backyard, if you are willing to look for it. Sometimes you'll discover that it was there all along, but you were just not paying attention.**

Kim and I love to take rides along the country roads of central Pennsylvania. It's a great way to unwind, re-connect, and talk without interruption. One of our favorite activities is to look at animals. There is a huge field about five miles away from our home that sits below an elementary school. Sometimes on the weekends during the summer, we will drive to the schoolyard and park, just before sunset. From our vantage point, we've counted as many as fifty deer at one time feeding in the field below. We've been doing this ever since we moved to our present home in 1997.

Shortly after completing my 25,000 bass pursuit, Kim and I went for a drive in the country. We only drove one street away from our daily path and discovered an enormous population of alpacas living on a farm less than three minutes from our front door. I don't know how long they have been there, but I do know that I have been so busy that I never bothered to look at what was just around the block.

How about you? What are you missing that is right under your nose?

I used to think that if I achieved fame and recognition from my bass fishing it would impress my wife. I stayed out for so many hours fishing for one more bass until my goal was met. The entire time I was away from the woman I love. One day, she stopped me dead in my tracks and said, *'I don't care about how many bass you catch. I'd rather you just be here spending time with me.'* And that was **the most important lesson of all-realign your priorities. Sometimes, the simple stuff can be the most significant things of all to those you love.**

Lesson: **It is better to be thought significant by one person whom you respect than to be thought significant by one thousand whose opinion you do not.** As the great author John Maxwell said, *'To change the world, you must first change yourself.'* **Is it time for you to change?**

***If your success is measured by how much
your accomplishments benefit you, then
your significance is measured by how much
your accomplishments benefit others.'***
– Dave Romeo

Chapter 22:
We May Never Pass this Way Again

'What we anticipate seldom occurs; what
we least expected generally happens.'
- Benjamin Disraeli

Many years ago, in the late seventies, I was dating a girl who lived in Oak Beach, New York. Oak Beach is a tiny little community which sits at the end of a sand bar located in Suffolk County on Long Island. In order to get there, I would cross over the southernmost Meadowbrook Parkway bridge to Jones Beach Island and drive approximately twelve miles across a long stretch of Ocean Parkway surrounded by deserted beaches, often in the dark. It allowed me the opportunity to be alone with my thoughts. Going there, my mind was filled with the anticipation of seeing this girl again. On the way home, I would drink in the fun of being in her company.

On one particular night, the drive home was completely occupied with inspiration from our most recent date. As I drove past all those abandoned sand dunes, I composed in my head the complete lyrics and music to an original song. By the time I returned home, it was very late so I couldn't play the song on my guitar until the next morning; yet it came out perfectly.

A similar experience happened while I was out there fishing that final year. The chapters of this still unwritten book were coming to me in waves as I continued to cast my way closer and closer to my goal. As a result, this reduced about a year and one-half of the usual three years it had taken to complete each of my previous three books. **I now believe it was the purpose for my bass fishing opus: to go learn all that was learnable so I could now teach all that is teachable.**

I thought I needed to fish to be who I am, but it turns out I needed to fish to get it out of my system so I could now become who I'm supposed to be. Thomas Wolfe declared, *'You can't go home again.'* While that might be true, *it doesn't mean you can't come home*. That's what I did: I freed myself from a twenty-seven-year-long pursuit so I could be the person I was destined to become. I don't think I could have arrived here in a more direct way without missing out on the experience of a lifetime. And as a result, *I can now reach you* through this book and beyond through the vehicle of e-mail and be a constant in your life for as long as I live. The accomplishments that may have brought us together mean relatively little to the people closest to me: my wife, my family, my friends, and my clients. No matter. The journey was tough. The rewards were worth it-to be able to sit in a chair and do a crossword puzzle; to sprawl out on a tarp-covered section of the family room floor and paint a statue; to embrace the stewardship of our property's greenery; to strum my *Cimar* acoustic guitar while safely out of anyone's earshot but my own; to watch a movie with my wife; or to sit out together on our deck drinking in the magnificent Elizabethtown, Pennsylvania sunset. These are priceless rewards that are much more greatly appreciated having committed to and accomplished some of my loftier goals.

Lesson: **What drives you? Why do you do the things you do? What makes something important or significant to you?**

In the pursuit of mastery, regardless of the exploit, my goal has always been to learn all that is learnable. With bass fishing, more specifically, my goal was to catch all that was catchable on any given day. Having accomplished that purpose, it was time to move on to make room to learn something else.

Probably one of the most common challenges many people in the free world face today is deciding what we want to do for a living. I'm not talking about a job. I'm talking about finding our calling. I know people in their sixties who still have not discovered what they want to do when they grow up.

Like most people who went to college, I couldn't find a job in my field of study (English). I was lucky to find a job as a bank teller, where I worked alongside history majors, business majors, and medical majors, none of whom were working in their respective fields.

Even though being a bank teller wasn't the job of my dreams, I knew that someday I would pursue my calling, which I had discovered while I went to college. And although it would take me another eighteen years after graduating to achieve that dream, I assure you it was well worth the wait. At one time, I intended to become an English teacher at the college level. When I shared my intentions with the English department dean, he said, *'We'd love to have you, but they'll have to carry one of us out of here feet first before there will be an opening.'*

Sure, it would have been nice to have been able to just walk into a teaching position with my alma mater right after I graduated; however, I see now that it never would have lasted for me. Allow me to explain why.

I don't know what your educational background is, but I can tell you that when I went to high school, I didn't take it seriously. It was just a place to go to be with my friends. But when I went to college, I took it very seriously because I was paying for my education-and, I must say, I was very disappointed. Most of my instructors didn't care if you lived or died. It didn't matter to them if you got an 'A' or an 'F.' One instructor, who bragged that he had gone to both Harvard and Yale, didn't make eye contact with anyone in our class for the entire semester.

Another very tall math instructor with a thick Brooklyn accent projected a very intimidating countenance. He was incredibly smart, but he would lose his temper, yell, and slam things if a student gave the wrong answer. I'd never before seen an entire classroom of students so gripped with the fear of making a mistake. He was brilliant with numbers and formulas; but he was completely ignorant when it came to inspiring people (except with fear).

Yet, that discouraging college experience would serve me well some eighteen years later when I became a seminar presenter. I remember thinking back then, that although my professors knew more than I did-I knew I could be a better teacher than those people. **They, like many educators in the United States, had forgotten that learning is supposed to be fun.** So, I decided that someday I would have my own classroom-not in some big, bureaucratic, regimented, sterile institution, but in a place where I could teach people *real-world* lessons that would help them grow both personally and professionally.

My dream was to have the people who attend my seminars feel like royalty from the moment they entered the room until the time they left. I would make it a point to know every person's name so I could involve him or her in the lesson plan. Each person would receive a personally handwritten thank-you card from me every time they attended one of my seminars.*

The royal treatment I have shown my seminar attendees has paid off immensely in so many ways, but it can best be summed up by a comment that one of my Hall of Fame-level clients, Jennifer Senft, once made. She said, *'You do things for me that my own mother wouldn't do.'* That's exactly how I wanted people to feel.

People would come to my seminars, not because they had to, but *because they sincerely wanted to be there and to learn.* That meant that many of them would be paying for their seminars out of their own pockets, over and over and over again, whether or not they had taken the seminar before and *regardless of the topic*. **They would come back because of the way I made them feel when they were in that room. In fact, I wanted them to feel so great by the time they left that they couldn't wait to come back for more.**

Have you ever heard someone say, 'If I get just one good idea from a seminar, it's worth it'? Well, **I made it my mission that no one who came to my seminar would leave *with just one* good idea.** My vision was to craft each lesson plan like I was designing the most delicious ice cream sundae that you ever tasted. It would consist of all your favorite flavors. Then I would cram in all of your favorite toppings so that every bite you took would be the best you ever tasted. I wanted people to be able to get a new breakthrough idea every five minutes.

And to make sure that every single seminar delivered that same desired impact, they all had to pass a three-prong criteria: they had to *entertain, enlighten, and inspire*.

I wanted people to feel so great, so appreciated, and so loved that by the end of my seminar, the first thing they would do is grab the seminar schedule and say, *'That was incredible! How soon is the next one?'*

I remember one of my clients, Dale Brown, after having attended just a handful of my seminars, making a statement as he introduced himself to the rest of the people attending a seminar on ***Legendary Customer Service***. He said, ***'I'm here today because I want my*** *customers to feel about me the way Dave Romeo's customers feel about him.'*

I wouldn't even have known this was possible to do had it not been for my good fortune to be a student in the elective classes of Professor Coffee starting in 1977. This was an experience unlike any others I had in college. Perhaps, you have heard the Chinese proverb that goes, **'When the student is ready, the teacher will appear.'** For me, Professor Coffee was that teacher. This man was incredibly gifted. He captivated his students and he made American history come alive through interesting and amusing anecdotes. I never knew that learning could be so invigorating until I experienced this master demonstrate how to do it.

Professor Coffee didn't just go through the motions. As a presenter now, I can appreciate how much additional research this educator had to do (**before** having access to the internet) to find such fascinating tidbits of historical trivia about famous figures in the American Revolution. I didn't even know that a teacher's delivery of American history could be so fascinating until this **seemingly insignificant** professor, in the span of two semesters, showed us how easy it was to accomplish.

I haven't seen Professor Coffee in thirty years. I doubt he would even know who I was or that I ever took any of his classes. All I know is, had it not been for his incredible example back in 1977 and 1978, I wouldn't have known what an inspirational teacher looked like or that such teachers even existed. How I wish that I could locate this great professor today and tell him what a profound impact he has made on my life and my career. If you should happen to run into this man, please let him know that he changed my life forever through his incredible gift of educational presentation mastery.

Lesson: **Your significance will not come directly from your accomplishments but from what they inspire others to do. My life would not have been the same were it not for that magnificent college professor. Through his example, I learned that one can choose whether or not to be 'ordinary.' Although he may never know how much I benefited from taking his classes, I will never forget how he set the bar so high on teaching. My tribute to him is to inspire you to do the same for others. What Professor Coffee did for me is what I hope to do for you-provide lessons on how to become significant in the hearts of the people whose lives you touch, even if you never know of all your successes.**

> *'If you keep growing, you will keep going.'*
> *- John Maxwell*

* After several years, this was modified to every first-time seminar attendee when one of my top-ten clients assured me that although she had attended twenty-nine seminars in one year, she didn't need twenty-nine thank-you cards. God love her for that!

Conclusion: The Last Cast

'Today is my best day!
- Mitch Robbins
(from 'City Slickers')

I remember reading an article in a bass fishing magazine many years ago about the last cast you make before you pack up and go home. The writer was trying to explain why the last cast is often so productive. Well, if there is one subject for which I feel qualified to comment, it would be on the last cast of the day. Any dedicated angler will tell you-you frequently catch a bass on the last cast of the day. I know I did.

Many times, I would promise my wife Kim that I would be back in the house by 8:00 PM. That meant I would be fishing against a deadline and cutting short many bass fishing excursions right at the day's peak productivity.

Your concentration becomes paramount. You put everything you have into the last cast because nothing else matters at that point. It's all on the line. It's all you can see. Your concentration, focus, and attention all combine to give you the greatest intensity of

the day. And it is in that final moment that we often discover who we are. The key is to put the same level of intensity into *every cast* as you put into *the last cast*. Make the most of each opportunity. Make each and every one count. Of course, you realize that I am not just referring to fishing.

Just like the rest of this book, *'the last cast'* is merely a metaphor for our lives. We pay the most attention to those moments when we feel everything is on the line. So we must learn to pack as much purpose into all of our days as if the next one might be our last. Here we are almost at the end of this book already and, yet, there is much more I wish to impart to you. So, let me pack as much into this chapter as I can as if it was the most important for you.

In bass fishing, as in business and in life, remember **there are two fundamental tracking tools to measure how you are doing. There are the actions you take and results you get. So, if you don't like the results you are currently getting, the only thing you can do is change your actions.**

When you approach your goal, whatever it may be, there are three things you must track if you want to get better. First, have a clear picture of where you want to end up. Next, know exactly where you are right now. And finally, look back to see how far you've already come. I have found this formula to be the most effective method of finishing what you start. And remember what that great sales trainer Brian Tracy says, *'You can never fail if you never give up.'*

Sophocles said, *'A man, though wise, should never be ashamed of learning more.'* What a great lesson! **Regardless of your passion, I challenge you to develop it to the point of mastery. You won't just be teaching people you know if you teach by example. You will be inspiring others who see or learn of you and your actions. They, in turn, can teach the lessons they learned from you to people who do not even know you. That is how you teach all that is teachable.**

Recently I met author Myron Golden for the very first time and he introduced me to *'The Law of Polarity.'* I had never heard of this law before, but Myron uses it as an excellent teaching tool in his fantastic book, *'From the Trash Man to the Cash Man.'* **The Law of Polarity means you can best explain what something is by contrasting it with its opposite.** For example, could you understand the concept of good without looking at evil? Would you understand the meaning of happiness without comparing it to sadness? How could you explain what success feels like without referring to failure? By the same token, starting out strong is nothing compared to finishing strong. I'll use the Law of Polarity to stress this lesson to you: *in a world of starters, be a finisher.* I assure you, you'll be in a very select group of people whom the world respects and admires.

Now, let me also use the Law of Polarity to point out my favorite definition of significance. If the benefits of your accomplishment are limited to you alone, that accomplishment may be viewed as insignificant. However, if your accomplishment results in a clear

and worthwhile purpose that benefits others as much as or more than it benefits you, your accomplishment has achieved significance.

I began writing this book in 2006, but I did not know at that time that it would be completed today, August 7, 2008, on my fiftieth birthday. Marking that milestone, it seems appropriate to reflect on the following quote by Adlai Stevenson which comes from an essay entitled, *'What a Man Knows at 50.'* I include this profound excerpt in my *'Approaching Change with a Positive Attitude'* seminar, but I believe it's worth sharing with you as well:

> *'What a man knows at 50, that he did not know at 20 is, for the most part, incommunicable.*
>
> *The knowledge he has acquired with age is not the knowledge of formulas or forms of words, but of people, places, actions-the knowledge not gained by words but by touch, sight, sound, victories, failures, sleeplessness, devotion, love-the human experiences and the emotions of this earth and of oneself and of other men; and perhaps, too, a little faith, a little reverence for things one cannot see.'*

What I have learned at fifty is that *there is no key to happiness. The door is always open.* You just have to be willing to walk through it once in a while.

Lesson: **The truest measure of significance you can contribute is a life worth emulating.** That's a life by which you have made yourself worthy of heaven. You will be leaving the world a legacy worth following. It won't always be easy but, as one of my clients Dawn Reese told me, *'When you find courage, you can make a difference.'* Show people through your example in all you think, do, and say, what it looks like to leave an eternal legacy. By doing so, striving for significance will become the reward you seek and a blueprint for others to follow.

Lesson: **Significance is not so much determined by the magnitude of your accomplishment but by the heart in which it lands. Pour yourself and your heart into each opportunity you take on and make it an effort worthy of emulation. Do it not just for yourself, but for anyone who is about to give up on a dream until that person learns about you. God gave you your life. You can thank Him by living it with meaning, purpose, and, of course, significance.**

As we conclude, I'll leave you with this revelation. As I look over the grounds of our modest home, I see our hill is in full bloom. The juniper we planted over ten years ago has spread like a bluish-green carpet which now blankets a fifteen-foot-high slope. Center-stage throughout is a sea of countless black-eyed Susans, displaying their magnificent brown and gold colors as far as you can see. The pink and white-colored Spirea bushes and the Cotoneaster shrubs (I only recently learned their names) have turned out very nicely, now that I've learned how to prune and shape them. What magic! And as I peer ever closer, I believe I spy some newly sprouted weeds. To think I once dreaded them so. What joy they bring me now, for I have a reason to once again throw myself into the greenery and become one with my newly-discovered passion. And how ironic that I used to be so anxious to escape this activity right under my own nose to pursue another. I see now that **one passion can be just as rewarding as another once you give yourself over to learn its life lessons.***

Charles Kingsley best summed up my feelings when he said, *'All we need to be really happy is something to be enthusiastic about.'* And I now understand the meaning of the saying, *'A peaceful heart finds joy in all of life's simple pleasures.'* **The pursuit of mastery knows no bounds.**

And now it's time to go out and walk the grounds. I wonder what I will discover this time.

> *'We do not climb the mountain because it is there.*
> *We climb it because we are here.'*
> *– Dave Romeo*

* If you have an observant eye, you may have been wondering about the photographic image on the spine of this book. It is a sliver of *'The Romeo Hill'* discussed in several chapters throughout this book. It is my plan to continue displaying the rest of the image across the spine of my next two books as they are completed. However, if you would like to see the entire image free-of-charge right now, e-mail me at <u>DaveRomeo@embarqmail.com</u> and request *'The Romeo Hill'* photo.

Be sure to watch for additional offers when you get on my e-mail list, and I thank you from the bottom of my heart for reading this book.

-- *Dave Romeo*

To Contact Dave Romeo

Dave Romeo serves as a personal and professional re-sults coach for people who are dissatisfied with their current results and are serious about doing something to improve them. His greatest areas of expertise are in accomplishing goals, achieving sales success, regaining focus, and developing accountability.

Dave also delivers motivational presentations guaran-teed to entertain, enlighten, and inspire. For a complete list of all available topics, please use the email address listed below to request a seminar menu.

All of these presentations and services are designed to produce positive results in the areas of both personal and professional growth and are 100% satisfaction guar-anteed.

Please contact Dave Romeo through the method be-low which offers you the greatest convenience.

Primary Seminars & Coaching
by Dave Romeo
1525 Oregon Pike, Suite # 501
Lancaster, PA 17601
Phone: (717) 569-9700 or (717) 361-2418
Fax: (717) 569-8620
E-mail: daveromeo@embarqmail.com
Web site: www.daveromeo.com
Web site: www.primarystaffing.com